Berlitz®

Japan

Front cover: Mt Fuji

Right: Woman from the Edo Period

TOP 10 ATTRACTIONS

Nara • Once Japan's first imperial capital, this city remains the country's cultural and artistic cradle (page 113)

Himeji • Home to the only castle in Japan that survives in its original form (page 144)

Kyoto • The city of temples, sanctuaries, geisha and Zen gardens has played a key role in the establishment of national identity (page 90)

Tokyo • Japan's capital is one of the largest cities in the world – it captures the tradition and futurism that is central to the magic of this extraordinary country (page 49)

Osaka • Japan's second city is a lively business and nightlife centre *(page 120)*

Mt Fuji • Nothing fully prepares the visitor for the sight of Japan's breathtaking national emblem *(page 87)*

Toshogu • The mausoleum at Nikko is the last resting place of Ieyasu, founder of the Tokugawa shogunate *(page 66)*

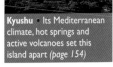

Kyushu • Its Mediterranean climate, hot springs and active volcanoes set this island apart *(page 154)*

Ise-Shima • This sacred area is renowned for its Shinto sanctuaries *(page 133)*

Nagasaki • Despite foreign influences, the city still has a strong Japanese flavour and much of its old town survived the atomic bomb *(page 169)*

CONTENTS

108

107

77

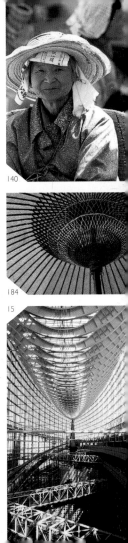

140

184

15

INTRODUCTION

Nihon-retto, the islands of the Japanese archipelago, were formed from the tears of a goddess. Where each tear fell into the Pacific there arose an island to take its place. So goes the legend. Today Japan is a country of astonishing contrasts: the rice farmers in rural heartlands and the subway millions of teeming Tokyo; the Zen Buddhist monks and the fad-obsessed teenage fashion victims; the solemn temple ceremony and the din of the pachinko parlour; exquisite temple architecture and concrete apartment buildings. All represent different facets of the greater whole that is Japan – one of the world's most intriguing countries.

The Japanese Archipelago

Japan lies on the Pacific Rim off the east coast of Asia. The archipelago consists of four main islands – Honshu, by far the largest, with Hokkaido to the north, Shikoku across the narrow Inland Sea and Kyushu to the southwest. In addition, about 3,900 smaller islands extend from southwest to northeast over a distance of some 3,800km (2,400 miles).

The main islands are noted for their rugged terrain, with 70 to 80 percent of the country being extremely mountainous. Most of the mountains that form the backbone of the Japanese archipelago were created over millions of years by the gradual collision of two of the earth's plates. Other peaks in Japan – including Fuji, the highest – are volcanic in origin. They were formed from molten lava from far below the earth's surface. Most of the country's mountains are covered in natural or plantation forest. The natural cover varies from subarctic conifers in Hokkaido, through deciduous and evergreen temperate broad-leafed trees on the other three main islands, to the subtropical forests of the islands of Okinawa in the far south.

A country of contrasts: green leaves against a vermilion pagoda

The city of Kagoshima, below Sakurajima's smoking summit

Japan's location on the Pacific 'Ring of Fire' means that the country experiences frequent earthquakes and volcanic activity. Earthquakes are far more frequent than volcanic eruptions, and the country suffers several extremely destructive quakes each century. One of the most recent was the powerful 1995 Hanshin earthquake, which destroyed much of the city of Kobe and killed over 6,000 people. Despite this danger, one of the top attractions for many visitors to Japan is the chance to see the milder geological forces in action. About 60 of Japan's 186 volcanoes are still active in geological terms, and occasionally they make their presence felt. Sakura-jima, on Kyushu and just a few kilometres from the city of Kagoshima, regularly spews ash – and an occasional boulder the size of a Honda – onto the city.

Most Japanese tend not to dwell on the hazardous aspects of the islands' geological activity, preferring to enjoy its pleasures instead. One big advantage of living on what amounts to a long string of volcanoes is the proliferation of *onsen,* or hot springs. For centuries hot springs have occupied a special place in Japanese culture, and now the pleasures of the onsen have become a national pastime. *Onsen* range from naturally occurring outdoor rockpools to large hotel-style resorts designed for guests to cast aside the stresses of the outside world as they soak for hours in communal hot tubs. Spending at least one night in a traditional Japanese inn-style *onsen* is an experience every visitor should enjoy.

A Crowded Nation

Despite the dominance of mountains, the Japanese are not a mountain people, preferring instead to squeeze onto the coastal plains or into the valleys of the interior. The jagged mountain ranges and dense forests leave less than two-fifths of the country suitable for habitation and most of Japan's 127 million people, factories, farmland, housing and public facilities are all crowded onto approximately 20 percent of the total land area. In terms of the ratio of population to usable land, Japan is the most densely populated country in the world.

The main industrial regions are the Kanto and Kansai areas, which are centred on Tokyo and Osaka respectively. Between these cities, towns and villages tend to merge into an indistinct urban blur that stretches endlessly across the flat land, with fields and farms dotted in between. Greater Tokyo now has a nominal population of almost 13 million, but in fact the city spreads beyond its political boundaries north, south and west to form a massive urban complex that stretches across the entire Kanto Plain. The actual population of this megalopolis is estimated at around 30 million people. The Kanto area alone produces nearly a third of Japan's entire gross domestic product.

Working the paddyfields

Visitors are impressed by how well people can co-exist in such a crowded country, and by the relative absence of violent street crime that plagues cities in so many other countries. Although crime rates are rising, Japan remains one of the safest countries in the world to live in or visit.

People

The Japanese population is relatively ethnically homogeneous – around 98 percent of the country's inhabitants are Japanese. From a mixture of Mongolian, Chinese, Korean

Throughout Japan, tradition and modernity sit side by side

and perhaps also Malay settlers, the country has had several thousand years to develop a solidly unified identity. Japan has never experienced large-scale immigration or even – until the postwar US occupation from 1945 to 1952 – foreign invasion.

But this does not mean Japanese society is free of discrimination. Many of the country's 700,000 Koreans have been residents of Japan for many generations, but Japanese law does not allow dual citizenship. Issues of identity remain complicated and many Koreans use Japanese names to avoid discrimination. The Ainu, an ethnically distinct community regarded by anthropologists as the islands' original settlers and now grouped almost exclusively in Hokkaido, campaign for civil rights in a movement similar to that of Native Americans in the US. The one million strong Okinawans, whose southern islands were only annexed by Japan in the 1870s, are also a distinct people with their own culture.

Another group, not of different ethnic origin from the Japanese mainstream but unquestionably inferior in status, are the *bura-*

kumin ('village dwellers', a euphemism for their old caste name – meaning 'much filth' – which was officially abolished at the end of the 19th century). They are descendants of outcasts employed to perform the originally taboo – and still disdained – trades of butchery, leatherwork, rubbish collection and the handling of corpses. Due to the stigma attached to their status, estimating the number of *burakumin* is tricky, but recent figures suggest that around 2 percent of the Japanese population falls into this category – anything from one to two million people. They live in separate hamlets or on city outskirts. You're most likely to come across them cleaning up litter in parks and temple grounds, or shining shoes at railway stations. For weeks after the Kobe earth-

Facts and Figures

Area: ranked 42nd largest country in the world, with 377,435 sq km (145,728 sq miles) of surface area on the four main islands (Hokkaido, Honshu, Kyushu and Shikoku) plus about 3,900 smaller islands. Mountains cover approximately 75 percent of the land. Highest point: Mt Fuji, at 3,776m (12,388ft).

Population: ranked 10th most populous in the world, with approximately 127 million Japanese, 540,00 Koreans, 800,000 Chinese and 130,000 other non-Japanese residents. Population density: 327 per sq km. Life expectancy at birth: 78 for males; 85 for females.

Capital: Tokyo (metropolitan population 12,800,000).

Major cities: Yokohama (3,600,000), Osaka (2,600,000), Nagoya (2,200,000), Sapporo (1,800,000), Kobe (1,500,000), Kyoto (1,470,000), Fukuoka (1,400,000), Kawasaki (1,300,000), Hiroshima (1,200,000) and Kita-Kyushu (1,000,000).

Government: Parliamentary democracy, headed by the Prime Minister and cabinet, with the emperor as titular head of state. Parliament (Diet) comprises the House of Representatives (480 seats) and the House of Councillors (247 seats). The country is divided into 47 prefectures, each with a governor.

quake in 1995, mounds of rubbish lay uncollected despite the quick resumption of other basic services. This was because one of the worst-hit districts was Nada-ku, a *burakumin* stronghold that suffered a high casualty and death toll.

Religion

Polls asking Japanese in which religion they believe consistently yield results that total well over 100 percent – most say they are followers of both Shinto and Buddhism. One of the main characteristics of Japanese religion is its tendency towards syncretism. Many people expect to have a Shinto baptism, a pseudo-Christian wedding (usually held in a hotel 'chapel' and officiated by an unordained foreigner in a robe) and a Buddhist funeral.

Quiet spirituality in hectic Tokyo

Shinto is the native religion of Japan, which influences virtually every aspect of Japanese culture and society. It is hard to give any simple definition of Shinto, since it is not a systematised set of beliefs. There is no dogmatic set of rules nor even any holy script. The term shinto was not even invented until after the introduction of Buddhism, a date traditionally given as AD552, and then only as a way of contrasting the native beliefs with that imported faith. Shinto is an animistic belief system involving the worship of *kami*, or spirits. Every living and non-living thing – animals, plants, rocks, mountains, the sun – contains a *kami*.

Buddhism arrived in Japan, via China and Korea, in the 6th century AD, but it didn't become popular until the 9th century. Over time, Buddhist thought became influenced by the indigenous beliefs of Shinto, so *kami* were regarded as temporary manifestations of the Buddhist deities. Quite often, Buddhist temples and Shinto shrines are found side by side, or a small temple will exist within the sacred grounds of a large shrine, or vice versa.

Extremes of Climate

Japan's climate varies widely, and its two extremities are in very different climatic zones. In the far north, Hokkaido experiences cool summers and icy winters. Deep snow banks develop between November and April and the island is known for its excellent skiing conditions. Honshu, the main island and home to the cities of Tokyo, Kyoto and Osaka, enjoys a temperate climate of unusually distinct seasons: bitter winters and hot, humid summers. The southern areas of Kyushu and Okinawa have a subtropical climate with mild winters and hot summers.

The coming of spring, manifested in the flowering of the country's swathes of cherry trees, is greeted with great excitement. The progress of the cherry blossom *(sakura)* from the south to the north is followed by the national media and celebrated with a festival called *hanami*. The cherry trees flower first in Kyushu towards the end of March; the phenomenon moves northward, typically reaching Hokkaido about the second week in May.

Temperatures rise quickly, and the continuous but moderate rains of *tsuyu*, the rainy season, begin to fall about two months after the end of the cherry-blossom season. The high mountain ranges running along the spine of Honshu define the boundaries of the rain fronts. On the Pacific Ocean coast, the tsuyu rain is soft and drizzly. Further south and on the Japan Sea coast, it is hard and much more tropical in nature. The rains ease around late June on the Pacific Ocean side and make way for the hot, humid summer. Temperatures reach a peak in August, when many city dwellers escape to the cool comfort of the mountains.

September sees the peak of the typhoon season. The southern or Pacific side of the country bears the brunt of these ferocious winds, which are quite capable of knocking down houses and wrecking ships. Generally three or four typhoons hit Japan during the season.

Architecture

Japanese builders have always had much to contend with – typhoons, earthquakes, floods and landslides all threaten to destroy their creations. The traditional building material is wood, particularly the wood of conifers, which is readily available from the forests that cover much of the country. The fact that Japan has the world's oldest wooden buildings (Horyu-ji, built about AD670 10km southwest of Nara) and the world's largest wooden structure (at Todai-ji in Nara, some 50m/165ft high and said to have been rebuilt at only two-thirds its original size) suggests that the architectural system adopted by the Japanese was at least partially successful in creating structures that last.

Traditional Japanese architecture combines box-shaped structures with heavy, elaborate roofs. Posts or columns bear the weight of the roof, so the walls could be thin and non-supporting. This was developed to the point that walls often ceased to be walls and became more like moveable partitions instead. Outside walls are often nothing more than a series of sliding wooden panels that can be easily removed, thus eliminating the solid border between inside and outside, a feature very much welcomed in Japan's humid summer. Carved and non-structural embellishment, especially on temples and other buildings that go in for opulent display, often shows a wild proliferation of scrolls, volutes and curvilinear motifs of many kinds, perhaps to offset the effect of this basic boxiness of the structure.

Japanese names

In Japan, the family name comes before the given name. The majority of people won't appreciate your using their given names unless you're a close acquaintance.

The materials used in traditional Japanese room interiors are simple and harmonious. Sliding panels are either made from translucent *shoji*, which allows soft light to diffuse in, or the heavier, opaque *fusuma* paper screens, or of wood. Floors are of thick, resilient straw mats surfaced with woven reed (*tatami* mats), or of plain wood. Supportive wooden posts remain exposed, and ceilings are generally of wood or of woven materials of various kinds. Wooden surfaces generally remain unpainted.

Japan has also embraced modern architecture and building materials, particularly in its largest cities. Materials such as glass tubing, gleaming metallic adjuncts, raw concrete, oxidized aluminium plates, translucent screens and fibre canopies are the order of the day. Futuristic structures incorporate hi-tech ventilating systems to heat and reuse air, roof-mounted solar-energy collectors, and wind walls to direct breeze flows to aerial courtyards and internal spaces, and there are plans afoot to use photo-voltaic glass to effectively turn buildings into power stations.

Futuristic lines in Tokyo

Tradition Meets Modernity

The constant clash between modern and traditional values leads to the numerous fascinating contradictions you will encounter in Japan. In its history, Japan has adopted many things, taking what it wants or needs, adapting, and then discarding that which is of no use. Over the centuries, the Japanese have adopted aspects of Chinese writing and philosophy, Korean art and ceramics, and most recently, Western technology, clothes and fast-food. Yet that which it adopts from the West or elsewhere somehow becomes distinctly Japanese.

As in centuries past, people go on mass pilgrimages to witness the spring blossoming of the famous cherry trees or the flaming golds, reds and ochres of the autumn maples. Nowadays, though, they travel via some of the world's most advanced transport systems, including the famous bullet trains *(shinkansen)* that zip through the countryside at over 300km (186 miles) per hour.

The centuries-old ceremony and ritual of a 15-day sumo-wrestling tournament is only enhanced by modern technology. The slow-motion instant replay of a pair of 150kg (330lb) sumo champions hurling each other across the ring with an *utchari* backward-pivot throw can be sheer poetry in motion.

Despite the concrete sprawl of Japan's postwar urban development, you can still find tranquillity in a brilliant-green, moss-covered temple garden or in the alcove of a traditional restaurant with its *tatami*-mat flooring, shielded from the other guests by *shoji* (paper screens) – remnants of a not-so-distant past.

Shinkansen trains are among the fastest in the world

The traditional Japanese family is both paternal (the man is nominally the household head) and maternal (as women still control the household budget and child rearing). However, the increasing empowerment of women outside the home has meant more financially independent females marrying later, or in many cases, not at all. Rather than stay in unhappy unions, many married couples have opted for separation. Soaring divorce rates have meant more single mothers.

Over this amazing cornucopia presides Emperor Akihito. Until 1946, his father Hirohito and all previous emperors were considered divinities, the living descendants of the gods who created Japan (or ancient Yamato, as it is more evocatively known). The emperor's role today is mainly symbolic, not unlike that of a modern European monarch. The imperial family remains largely out of sight, never giving opinions on matters of state or politics, wholly removed from the daily life of their subjects.

The best way to gain an understanding of Japan is to open your eyes, your ears and, of

Decorative Buddhist gong in Nara temple

course, your mind. Savour the delicacy of the cuisine, a feast for all the senses. Take in the formal beauties of *kabuki* theatre, Zen rock gardens and *ikebana* flower arrangements; struggle to stay awake through an entire *noh* performance. Participate in the graceful tea ceremony or watch the dazzling display of skill in *kendo* (stick fighting), with its impressively fierce battle cries.

Few visitors will come to Japan truly free of preconceptions. Japan is a country where the intriguing, the exotic and the utterly baffling are commonplace, where little can be taken at face value. Yet few people are so warmly welcoming of strangers as the Japanese. Ultimately, visitors who remain open-minded and ready for adventure will be rewarded by unexpected and unforgettable experiences available nowhere else on the planet.

A BRIEF HISTORY

According to the earliest official accounts, the 8th-century *Kojiki* ('Record of Ancient Matters') and *Nihon-shoki* ('Chronicles of Japan'), the islands of Japan were born of a marriage between the god Izanagi and his sister Izanami. They also – but only later – gave birth to the sun, in the form of the goddess Amaterasu, who endowed the Japanese imperial family with its regalia of bronze mirror, iron sword and jewel. The mirror is kept to this day at the Shinto shrine of Ise-Shima.

Before you dismiss all this as the mere 'myth' of Japan's origins, remember that the Japanese continued to trace the imperial dynasty directly back to those deities until Emperor Hirohito in 1946 denounced 'the false conception that the emperor is divine'. Although these creation myths still appeal to the popular imagination, few Japanese people accept them as historical fact, and only a tiny minority still believe the Emperor to be a divine figure.

The Ainu

The Ainu (meaning 'human'), whose current population numbers fewer than 20,000, were the first inhabitants of Hokkaido and the north of Honshu. Their origins remain unknown. They were once thought to be of Caucasian descent, but more recent studies of blood and bone samples link them to the peoples of Siberia.

Prehistory and Early Chronicles

As evidenced by bones, weapons and pottery most recently uncovered by archaeologists, humans first crossed a now-submerged land bridge from eastern Siberia to what is now Sakhalin Island and northern Japan some 100,000 years ago. These migrants, who later settled throughout the Japanese archipelago, were the ancestors of the present-day Ainu, whose Caucasoid facial and body hair distinguished them from subsequent immigrants from China, Manchuria, Korea and perhaps the Malay Peninsula. It was the growth and military assertion of the newcomers that drove the 'hairy people' (as they were labelled) north to their present concentration in Hokkaido.

The oldest Stone Age settlements to be discovered (10,000BC) are known as Jomon ('cord pattern'), after the style of their handmade pottery, which was among the earliest to be found anywhere in the world and of rich and imaginative design. Their inhabitants dwelt in sunken pits and made a living from hunting, fishing and the gathering of roots and nuts. It wasn't until

Clay figure from the Jomon Period

the 3rd century BC that techniques of rice cultivation (and wheel-made pottery) arrived from Korea, along with irrigation methods that are still in use today.

The scarcity of flatlands suitable for cultivation made it possible for a small aristocratic élite to gain quick control of the food resources. This set the pattern of hierarchical rule that was to prevail right up to the last half of the 19th century (some would claim, in economic terms at least, that it still persists today).

Although there are no reliable accounts of this period, 3rd-century Chinese documents speak of a Japanese priestess-queen, Himiko, ruling over a land of law-abiding people who enjoyed alcohol and were divided into classes distinguished by tattoo marks. Five centuries later, Japan's own *Kojiki* and *Nihon-shoki* chronicles describe the creation of the imperial dynasty in the year 660BC: the first emperor, Jimmu ('Divine Warrior') – great grandson of the Sun Goddess's grandson – embarked on an expedition of conquest from Kyushu along the Inland Sea coast to the Yamato plain of the Kinki region (near modern-day Nara).

Plausible chronicling, laced with a dose of mythology, begins with the arrival of Korean scribes at the Japanese court around AD400, at a time when Japan also had a military foothold in southern Korea. The state of Yamato, as early Japan was known, was organised into *uji*, or clusters of clans, together with subordinate guilds of farmers, fishermen, hunters, weavers and potters, all subject to the dominant *uji* of the imperial family.

The Way of the Gods

The major tenets of Shinto – Japan's indigenous religion – were the imperial family's direct descent from the Sun Goddess and the resulting divinity of the emperor. Although his divinity was renounced only after World War II, the emperor remains Shinto's titular head.

Literally 'the way of the gods', Shinto has a strong component of nature-worship, with shrines in such places of great natural beauty as mountain tops or forests, where divine spirits are believed to inhabit waterfalls, unusual rocks or great trees. Its followers respect the deities through ritual purification ceremonies. Menstruation, childbirth, sickness, injury and death are all considered sources of impurity – workers in slaughterhouses, tanneries or graveyards have traditionally been restricted to a caste of 'untouchables', now known as the *burakumin*.

Shinto remains a less solemn religion than Westerners are used to. The commercial bustle around Tokyo's Asakusa shrine evokes the atmosphere of a Western country fair. At the shrine, people clap their hands to attract the gods' attention, bow respectfully, toss coins into a slotted box and offer up prayers. Then they visit the food stalls, amusement booths and souvenir shops located inside the sanctuary grounds. In few countries do religion and commerce coexist so harmoniously.

Chinese Influences

The Japanese were forced out of the Korean peninsula in the 6th century, but not before the Koreans had bequeathed to the Yamato court copies of the sacred images and scriptures of Chinese Buddhism.

Just as Christianity introduced Mediterranean culture into northern Europe, so Buddhism brought Chinese culture into Japanese society. Throughout the 7th and 8th centuries numerous Japanese monks, scholars and artists made the perilous trip west across the Sea of Japan to

Prince Shotoku developed the country's first constitution

study Chinese religion, history, music, literature and painting – later to be brought back for further development in Japan.

An outstanding figure of this time was Prince Shotoku, who in 604 developed the 'Seventeen-Article Constitution', outlining a code of human conduct and the ideals of state as a basic law for the nation. He also established relations with the Sui dynasty in China. Through him, the Japanese imperial court developed Chinese patterns of centralised government, with its formal bureaucracy of eight court ranks. The Chinese calendar was used to calculate the year of Japan's foundation by counting back the 1,260 years of the Chinese cosmological cycle. Thus, 660BC is still the official date, celebrated nationwide on 11 February.

At this early stage in its history Japan was already (for the most part) only nominally ruled by the emperor. *De facto* power was exercised by the militarily and economically strongest family. The Sogas had promoted Buddhism as an imperially sanctioned counterweight to the native Shinto religion, along with the new Chinese

An exquisite golden buddha from Nara's Todaiji Temple

customs, to weaken the influence of their more conservative rivals. But they in turn were ousted in AD645 by Naka-tomi Kamatari, founder of the great Fujiwara clan, which was to rule Japanese affairs for hundreds of years and provide prominent advisers to the emperor even up to the 19th century.

The Nara Period

Another of the new ideas was to set up a permanent residential capital for the imperial court, initially at Naniwa (present-day Osaka) and then a little to the east, at Nara, in 710. Laid out like a chessboard (nearly half the size of China's similarly designed capital, Chang'an), Nara had its imperial palace at the northern end, with court residences, Buddhist monasteries and Shinto shrines stretching to the south. In those peaceful years, without threat of foreign invasion or civil war, there were no city ramparts.

The era known as the Nara Period was marked by the religious fervour of the Buddhist monks and also by their accompanying artistic achievements. The Japanese were attracted more to Buddhism's ritual and art than to its complex philosophy, rendered all the more difficult because its texts were, for several centuries, available only in Chinese, the language of a small court élite. Buddhist monks initiated great progress in Japanese architecture, bronze-casting, bridge-building and sculpture. To this day, historians of Chinese art find the best surviving examples of Tang-dynasty architecture among the 7th- and 8th-century temples in and around Nara.

The imperial government achieved tight control, with administrative power centralised in a grand council. All land used for rice cultivation was claimed to be under imperial ownership, a state of affairs that later led to heavy taxation of farmers.

The Fujiwara clan dominated. By marrying his daughters to sons of the reigning emperor and then engineering timely abdications, a Fujiwara contrived always to be father-in-law, uncle or grandfather behind the throne. Very often the emperor was only a minor, so that the Fujiwara patriarch acted as regent. He then persuaded the emperor to abdicate soon after his majority, and the regency would continue for the next youthful incumbent. The important thing was to have the emperor's sanction for the regent's political decisions.

Very few emperors were reluctant to submit to Fujiwara domination. The burden of his spiritual functions as high priest of Shinto and the tasks of administration led the emperor to welcome an early abdication, frequently to retire to a life of Buddhist meditation and scholarship. The Fujiwara resented the Buddhist clergy's great and growing influence in imperial affairs. There were too many monasteries in and around Nara. It was time to move the capital.

The Golden Heian Era

The geomancers in 794 decided that Heian-kyo (modern Kyoto) would be an auspicious site for the imperial family. It was indeed – until 1869.

Grants of tax-free land over the years had been made to Buddhist temples and members of the court aristocracy. The most powerful families thus carved out for themselves whole regions that were to become the fiefdoms of Japanese feudalism. By the end of the 8th century the clans had created a hierarchy of *shiki,* or rights, from the highest to the lowest ranks of society. The aristocrat or court patron lent his prestige to a powerful provincial proprietor, who employed a competent estate-manager to oversee smallholders, who in turn worked their farms with dependent labourers. This elaborate structure of interdependent rights and obligations was to serve Japanese society right into the 20th century.

Meanwhile, Heian court life blossomed in an effusion of aesthetic expression. Princes and princesses judged the merits of birds, insects, flowers, roots or seashells. Literary party games held in ornate palace gardens required each guest to compose a small poem as his wine cup floated towards him along a miniature winding channel of water. Expeditions were organised to the best viewing points for the first spring cherry blossoms and special pavilions were built to watch the rising of the full moon. Every gesture, from the most banal opening of an umbrella to the sublimest act of lovemaking, had its appropriate ceremonial. Conversation often took the form of elegant exchanges of improvised verse.

Ancient illustration from *The Tale of Genji*

The changing role of Chinese culture in Japanese life was epitomised in the language itself. In the absence of an indigenous alphabet, Japanese scholars had with the greatest difficulty tried to adapt the complex ideograms of monosyllabic Chinese to the essentially polysyllabic Japanese. Thus developed the *katakana* system used as a vehicle for writing Buddhist names and concepts.

> ### The Tale of Genji
>
> *The Tale of Genji*, a major work of Japanese classical literature, was written in the early 11th century by the daughter of a courtier. The book chronicles the exciting amorous adventures of the handsome Genji, a Heian-period courtier.

Provincial areas were neglected by the imperial court. Banditry became widespread and local administrators were more interested in personal gain than in enforcing law and order. The result was that the lords of great estates developed their own miltary power.

After rival Fujiwara factions had been struggling for years to gain control of the imperial throne, they turned to the Taira and Minamoto armies in 1156 to wage the four-year war that heralded the end of the golden age of the Heian court. The Taira, controlling the region along the Inland Sea, defeated the Minamoto armies based in the Kanto province east of the capital.

Over the next 20 years, the Minamoto clan acquired new strength by offering better guarantees to local landowners – and their armies – than they could expect from court. Eventually a new offensive, the decisive Gempei War, was launched in 1180. Five years later, the Taira were overthrown after being defeated in the straits between western Honshu and Kyushu, at the titanic sea battle of Dannoura – which has a place in Japanese annals comparable to Waterloo or Stalingrad.

Enter the Shoguns

Japan's austere, ruthless, but statesmanlike new ruler, Yoritomo Minamoto, set up his government in Kamakura (just south of modern Tokyo), well away from the 'softening' influence of court life that had been the undoing of his predecessor, Kiyomori. First of the national rulers to take the title of *sei-i tai-shogun* ('barbarian-subduing great general'), Minamoto expanded and consolidated his power by confiscating lands from some of the defeated Taira and redistributing them to his *samurai* (warrior-caste) vassals.

Minamoto died in 1199, and the feudal structure passed intact to the tutelage of his widow's family, the Hojo, who were content to play regent to a figurehead shogun, in much the same way as the Fujiwara had done with the emperor. The fiction of Japanese imperial power had become infinitely extendable. The emperor at Kyoto – still seconded by a Fujiwara regent at court – legitimised a Minamoto who was himself a military dictator controlled by a Hojo regent. In a country where form and substance were inextricably interrelated, two things counted in politics: symbolic authority and real power. Neither could exist without the other.

Although the Kamakura Period was relatively brief, there were events and developments that profoundly affected the country. A revolutionary advance in agricultural techniques occurred that allowed greater production of food. Consequently, there was a significant increase in population and economic growth, with more intense settlement of the land, better commerce and trade, the growth of local markets, and the beginnings of a currency system. Contact with the Chinese mainland resumed on a private basis.

A thwarted Mongol invasion in 1274 weakened the Kamakura regime. The fighting brought none of the usual spoils of war that provincial warlords and samurai had come to expect as payment. And the treasury was empty after earthquake, famine and plague had crippled the economy. Buddhist monasteries were using their private armies to support imperial ambitions to bring power back to Kyoto. Worst of all, the Kamakura warriors, resenting the way the Kyoto court referred to them as 'Eastern barbarians', sought refinement in a ruinous taste for luxury: extravagant feasts, rich costumes and opulent homes. Kamakura was falling apart.

Creative Turmoil

The subsequent power struggle at first split the country into two imperial courts, and then effective control of Japan was splintered for two centuries among scores of *daimyo* (feudal warlords). Eventually, the Ashikaga family of shoguns settled down in Kyoto's Muromachi district, which gave its name to the new creative period that followed. The gruff, bluff warriors' taste for art – calligraphy, landscape painting, the tea ceremony, music, dance and theatre – coincided with a renewed interest in things Chinese, above all the

The *shogun* Yoritomo Minamoto set up his regime at Kamakura

teachings of Zen Buddhism. Although Zen had been present in Japan since the 12th century, its ascendancy began under the Kamakura regime, which found the mystic Chinese philosophy admirably suited to Japanese sensitivity, impressionism and love of form and ritual.

The Ashikaga shoguns and their samurai were greatly attracted by an essentially anti-intellectual doctrine that transmitted its truth from master to disciple by practical example rather than scholarly study of texts. Enlightenment *(satori)* was to be achieved through self-understanding and self-discipline, combining tranquillity and individualism. After their savage battles, the warriors recuperated through meditation in the peace of a Zen monastery rock garden.

Other important developments occurred at this time. Agricultural techniques were improved, new crops were introduced, and irrigation and commercial farming expanded. Guilds of specialised craftsmen appeared, a money economy spread, and trade increased markedly. Most importantly, towns and cities arose and grew; such development was accompanied by the appearance of merchant and service classes.

A *samurai* in full battle regalia

The assassination of an Ashikaga shogun in 1441 started the decline of the shogunate; the relationship between the shogun and the military governors of the provinces broke down. A decade of war and unrest marked the total erosion of centralised authority and a general dissolution of society. It ushered in the Age of Warring States, a century of civil war that lasted from 1467 until 1568.

Battles raged up and down the country among some 260 daimyo, from which a dozen finally emerged victorious. They had fought with mass armies of infantry rather than relying on the old cavalry élite. Although swords and bows and arrows remained the mainstays of warfare, suddenly matchlocks, muskets and cannons made their appearance. The Europeans had arrived.

In 1543 Portuguese explorers reached Tanegashima Island, off southern Kyushu, followed over the next decade by Portuguese traders and Jesuit missionaries, headed by St Francis Xavier, who landed at Kagoshima in 1549. Many Kyushu daimyo adopted

Christianity as a means of winning favour with the Portuguese traders, without necessarily abandoning their Buddhist beliefs or Shinto practices. Converted nine years earlier, daimyo Omura founded the port of Nagasaki as a centre for Portuguese trade in 1571. The town was handed over to the Jesuits in 1579. By 1582, Christian converts were estimated at 150,000; by 1615 there were half a million throughout the country. (Through all the vagaries of persecution and war, Nagasaki has remained the major centre of Japanese Christianity.)

Trade with the Portuguese – and the Dutch – launched a craze for tobacco, bread, potatoes, clocks, pantaloons and eyeglasses, the latter very often worn as a chic symbol of intellectual superiority rather than as an aid for poor eyesight.

Momoyama Unification

By 1568, when Kyoto was at last seized from the Ashikaga shogunate, three ruthless generals – Nobunaga, Hideyoshi and Tokugawa – had banded together to eliminate all remaining opposition. Realising the importance of Western military technology, Nobuna-

The Way of the Samurai

The way of the samurai – *bushido* – was a most serious path to follow, 'a way of dying' to defend the honour of one's lord or one's own name. Often that meant *seppuku*, or ritual disembowelment. An unwritten code of behaviour and ethics, *bushido* came to the foreground during the Kamakura period.

In the Edo period, *bushido* helped to strengthen *bakufu*, or the shogunate government, by perfecting the feudal class system of samurai, farmer, artisan and merchant. The ruling samurai class was by far the most powerful in Japan.

Only when the economy shifted from rice-based to monetary did the merchants take control of Edo (Tokyo), and the samurai fell increasingly into debt.

Osaka Castle, built by Hideyoshi and burnt down by Tokugawa Ieyasu, is testament to its own turbulent history

ga mastered the manufacture of gunpowder and made firearms from melted-down temple bells. The triumphant trio were the first to develop the appropriate defences against the new firepower. They replaced the old small castles on high ground protected only by wooden stockades with large central fortresses out of range behind broad moats, surrounded by solid stone ramparts and earthworks strong enough to resist cannon fire.

Cleverest of the three, Nobunaga used another Western weapon, Christianity, against the principal remaining threat to his authority – the strongholds surrounding Kyoto. While sending out armies to destroy the Buddhist monasteries and confiscate their lands, he simultaneously fostered Christianity to win adepts away from the Buddhist faith.

Nobunaga was assassinated by one of his own generals in 1582, and Hideyoshi, who had started out as a simple infantryman, succeeded him. Seeing in Christianity a threat to his central authority, Hideyoshi systematically suppressed Christian activity; in 1597 six missionaries and 20 Japanese converts were crucified at Nagasaki. He was also a master of the art of conspicuous consumption, contrasting sharply with the restraint shown by the Ashikaga shoguns in their more subtle displays of wealth. The gigantic castle he erected at Osaka was the biggest Japan had ever seen, requiring a work force of 30,000 men. Perhaps his most astounding coup was the monstrous Kitano tea ceremony attended by hundreds of rich and poor followers, who were all obliged to stay to the end. It lasted 10 days.

Hideyoshi made two attempts to conquer Korea in 1592 and 1597 with the aim of taking over China. His death in 1598 brought this megalomaniacal effort to a swift end.

The cultural achievements of the three decades since the end of the Ashikaga shogunate were astonishing. The country was in political ferment, yet glorious textiles, ceramics and paintings were produced.

Tokugawa Takes All

When Hideyoshi died, he hoped his five-year-old son would continue his 'dynasty', initially under the tutelage of five regents. But one of the regents was Tokugawa Ieyasu, who had been biding his time at Edo (now modern-day Tokyo) for 12 years, nurturing dynastic ambitions of his own. Of the cunning, ruthless triumvirate that came out on top at the end of the country's century of civil war, Tokugawa was without doubt the most patient, the most prudent – and most treacherous. He moved quickly to eliminate his strongest rivals, crushing them in 1600 at the great Battle of Sekigahara (near modern Nagoya) and became Japan's *de facto* ruler. In 1603, Tokugawa Ieyasu was given the title of shogun by the still subservient but symbolically important emperor.

During its subsequent two and a half centuries of rule from the new capital established at Edo, the Tokugawa clan organised a tightly controlled coalition of some 260 daimyo located in strategic strongholds throughout the country. The allegiance of this highly privileged and prestigious group was ensured by

Monument to the Christian
martyrs, Nagasaki

cementing their ethical principles in the code of *bushido*, 'the way of the warrior': loyalty to one's master, defence of one's status and honour, and fulfilment of all obligations. Loyalty was further enforced by holding the vassals' wives and children hostage in Edo. All roads into Edo, the most famous being the Tokaido Highway, had checkpoints for guns coming in and for wives going out.

One of the most effective ways of keeping a tight rein on the country was to cut it off from the outside world, to keep Japan Japanese. At first, Tokugawa Ieyasu was eager to promote foreign trade. He wanted silk and encouraged the Dutch and British as good, non-proselytising Protestants just interested in trade. But he didn't like the Portuguese and Spanish Catholic missionaries, who he felt were undermining traditional Japanese values. He banned their activities in 1612 and two years later ordered the expulsion of all Christian missionaries and unrepentant Japanese converts. Executions and torture followed. Converts were forced to renounce their faith by trampling crucifixes and effigies of Jesus and Mary. The Catholic Church has counted 3,125 martyrs in Japan from 1597 (beginning under Hideyoshi) to 1660.

Japan closed itself off from the world. In 1635 the Japanese were forbidden, on pain of death, to attempt to travel abroad and Japanese citizens already overseas were prevented from returning, in case they brought back subversive Christian doctrines. Western books were banned, as were Chinese books that mentioned Christianity. After the purge of foreigners, only a few stayed on, strictly confined to Dejima Island in Nagasaki Bay.

This isolation slowed Japan's technological and institutional progress almost to a halt. But it also had the effect of permitting a great, distinctive cultural growth with a strong national identity. The Tokugawa thus celebrated the ancestral religion of Shinto – glorified by the monumentally opulent shrines they built at Nikko. Combining Shinto ritual with official Buddhist conformity, they revived the Confucian ideals of filial piety and obedience to authority to bolster the authority of their government. Whether in Edo or the countryside, every person knew exactly what his or her position in society was and of how they were to behave. People in a daimyo's domain had little recourse if their lord was autocratic, unprincipled or arbitrary.

Long years of isolated peace slowly replaced the warrior's importance with that of the merchant. Commerce thrived, partly in response to the extravagant demands of the Tokugawa court. Mer-

Buddhism – Japanese Style

Buddhist philosophy originated in India c.500BC. Pure Buddhist doctrine teaches the quest for enlightenment (nirvana) by the progressive abandonment of desire, the source of all life's pain. In Japan, Buddhist practice shifted away from private contemplation to public charity work. The requirements of celibacy and asceticism were also gradually dropped.

For the Japanese, Buddhism initially appealed as a protector of both the state and the noble families, who built temples near their homes. New sects in the 9th century spread Buddhism throughout the country. The religion evolved from protector of the aristocracy to vehicle of faith and hope for the common people, who were attracted by the prayers and elaborate rituals.

By the 12th century Buddhism had integrated with the indigenous Shinto religion. It was also suffused with those elements of Chinese Confucianism appropriate to the Japanese character: family solidarity, filial piety and loyalty to the ruler and to authority in general. As always, the Japanese proved to be not slavish imitators but ingenious adapters.

The fleet of Commodore Matthew Perry

chants thronged to the large cities that were growing up around the castles at Edo (population already 1 million in the 18th century), Osaka (400,000) and Nagoya and Kanazawa (each 100,000). In 1801, when Britain's navy dominated the seas, Europe's largest city, London, had fewer than a million inhabitants. Japan's overall population in the 18th century was already about 30 million.

Merchants played an active role in creating the distinctive urban culture that burgeoned at the end of the 17th century, the so-called Genroku era. Before these hard-working family men went home from work, they liked to drink strong alcohol in the company of actresses and prostitutes. These were the forerunners of the geisha – literally 'accomplished person' – with a beauty and refinement that the merchants did not seek in their wives, whom they valued for their childbearing and good housekeeping. These were also halcyon days for the classic *noh* theatre, the more popular *kabuki* and the puppet theatre (today's *bunraku*) at Osaka, which was Japan's cultural capital at a time when Edo had more politicians and soldiers than artists.

In the end it was the very rigidity of their unshared control of the country that brought about the downfall of the Tokugawa. Without access to foreign markets, there was no way to counter the rash of catastrophes – plague, drought, floods and famine – at the end of the 18th century. Uprisings in the towns and countryside began to pose serious threats to the shogun's authority. The Tokugawa reaction was characteristic: a reinforcement of the austere values of the samurai and a rigorous clamp-down on the merchants' high life. There was no more gambling, prostitutes were arrested, and men and women were segregated in the public bathhouses, with naked government spies to enforce the (short-lived) new rules.

The Yankees Are Coming

The feeling began to grow that the only way out of the crisis was to open the country to foreign trade and new ideas. The Tokugawa shoguns, however, sensed that the internal strains might be contained, by sheer brute force if necessary, as long as new pressures were not exerted from outside by foreigners once again offering disgruntled daimyo new sources of income. At the same time, the industrial revolution was gaining momentum in Europe. The Western powers were casting about for more countries into which to expand economic influence.

While others had tried rattling Japan's doors, it was the United States that yanked them open in 1853 with Commodore Matthew Perry and America's East India Squadron – the famous 'Black Ships'. Perry delivered to the shogun (whom he mistook for the emperor) a polite but insistent letter from President Millard Fillmore and a promise to return the next year, with a bigger squadron, for a positive response.

In 1854 Perry negotiated the Treaty of Kanagawa, opening

What year is it?

Japan uses two methods for indicating the year: the Western system (ie 2009) and a system based on how long the current emperor has reigned (ie Heisei 21). The latter appears frequently on official documents.

Woman from the Edo Period, in colourful kimono

up two ports, Shimoda on the Izu Peninsula and Hakodate in Hokkaido. Similar treaties were signed with Britain and Russia. The West had driven in the thin end of its wedge. More and more ports were opened to foreign trade, and the Japanese were obliged to accept low import tariffs.

As the Tokugawa shoguns had feared, this opening of the floodgates of Western culture after such prolonged isolation had a traumatic effect on Japanese society. The Tokugawa had successfully persuaded the samurai that traditional values might suffer, and now the samurai felt betrayed, rallying under the slogan 'Sonno joi!' ('Honour the emperor, expel the barbarians!').

Before they could even think of accepting contact with the outside world, national integrity had to be restored, under the renewed moral leadership of the emperor. Samurai assassinated British and Dutch representatives. In 1863, the daimyo of Choshu (in western Honshu) fired on foreign ships in the Shimonoseki Straits. In response, the Americans, British, Dutch and French combined forces to smash the Choshu fortified positions, and Britain retaliated for the assassination by almost levelling Kagoshima in southern Kyushu. The local daimyo of Satsuma was so impressed that he started to buy British ships, which became the foundation of the future Imperial Japanese Navy.

The Meiji Restoration

In 1868 the Satsuma and Choshu clans, never a real threat to Tokugawa authority as long as they remained rivals, joined forces to overthrow the shogun and restore the authority of the emperor, the 14-year-old Mitsuhito. Edo was renamed Tokyo ('Eastern Capital'), and Mitsuhito took over the Tokugawa castle as his palace.

But important though the resuscitated imperial authority undoubtedly was, the real power under the restoration known as *Meiji* ('Enlightened Rule') was in the hands of a new generation of forward-looking administrators, who set about abolishing the ancient feudal apparatus in favour of a modern government based on merit rather than ancestry. They emphasised the need to acquire Western military and industrial skills and technology with which to confront the West itself and eliminate unfair trade tariffs and other unjust aspects of the foreign treaties.

Agriculture, commerce and traditional manufacturing were expanded to provide a sound economic base for investment in the modern technology of textiles and other industries. Shipbuilding and weapons manufacture were already under way; railways and telegraph lines quickly followed. And to show just how fast Japan's new rulers were catching on, two punitive expeditions were launched against Korea and China in the grand manner of 19th-century gunboat diplomacy.

There was an inevitable reaction to rapid Westernisation. Traditional Japanese theatre, the tea ceremony, *ikebana* flower arrangement and the old martial arts all came back into

Emperor Mitsuhito promulgating the Meiji constitution

favour. In 1890 an important imperial edict on education was is-
sued, promoting Asian (that is, Chinese and Japanese) values in
culture and stressing loyalty to the emperor and general harmony.
If the singing in school of military songs such as 'Come, Foes,
Come!' or 'Though the Enemy Be Tens of Thousands Strong' seems
excessively belligerent today, we should not forget jingoistic atti-
tudes in Europe and America at the time.

Japan made a dramatic debut on the international stage, with
military actions against China and Russia. The 1894 Sino-
Japanese War for control of the Korean markets and the strategic region of southern Manchuria was a triumph for Japan's
modernised army over China's larger but much less well-organ-
ised forces. More impressive still was Japan's success against the
powerful war machine of Czarist Russia (1904–1905), beginning with a surprise nighttime attack on the Russian fleet, to be
repeated some years later at Pearl Harbor. The West was forced
to accept Japan's occupation of southern Manchuria and the an-

Tokyo in the 1930s

nexation of Korea in 1910. In just 40 years, Japan had established itself as a viable world power.

Triumph and Disaster

The 20th century saw a stupendous release of energies that had been pent up for the 250 years of Tokugawa isolation. By 1930 raw-material production had tripled the figure of 1900, manufactured goods had increased 12-fold and heavy industry was galloping towards maturity. Britain led the World War I allies in large orders for munitions, while Japan expanded sales of manufactured goods to Asian and other markets cut off from their usual European suppliers. Merchant shipping doubled in size and increased its income 10-fold as the European fleets were destroyed.

Setbacks in the 1930s caused by the European postwar slump were only a spur to redouble efforts by diversifying heavy industry into the machine-making, metallurgical and chemical sectors. Even the terrible 1923 Tokyo earthquake, which cost over 100,000 lives and billions of pounds, provided another stimulus due to the construction boom that followed.

Riding the crest of this economic upsurge were the *zaibatsu* conglomerates – a dozen family-run combines, each involved in mining, manufacturing, marketing, shipping and banking. These tightly controlled commercial pyramids were the true heirs to the old feudal structures.

Japan's progress towards parliamentary democracy was halted in the 1930s by the growing nationalism being imposed on government by the generals and admirals. They proclaimed Japan's mission to bring progress to its backward Asian neighbours in language not so very different from that of the Europeans in Africa or the US in Latin America. After the Russian Revolution of 1917, the Soviet Union was regarded as a major threat to Japan's security, and the army felt it needed Manchuria and whatever other Chinese territory it could control as a buffer against Russian advances. In 1931 the Japanese occupied Manchuria. And then in 1937, with the popular support of ultra-right-wing groups, the army overrode parliamentary resistance in Tokyo and went to war against the Chinese Nationalists. The Japanese campaign against the Chinese was brutal – in the occupation of Nanking, for example, troops slaughtered from 150,000 to 300,000 civilians. By 1938, the Japanese held Nanking, Hankow and Canton.

Japanese expansionist policies were leading to direct confrontation with the West. Japan hoped that war in Europe would divert the Soviet Union from interference in East Asia, giving Japan a free hand both in China and, through its alliance with Germany, in French Indochina after the defeat of France. The US responded to the Japanese invasion of Indochina with a trade and fuel embargo, cutting off 90 percent of Japan's supplies. The result was the attack on the American fleet at Pearl Harbor (7 December 1941) and total war.

Early successes in the Philippines, Borneo, Malaya, Singapore and the Dutch East Indies enabled Japan to establish the so-called Greater East Asia Co-Prosperity Sphere. The 'liberation' of these old European colonies created the basis for postwar independence movements proclaiming the Japanese slogan 'Asia for the Asians'. Despite this, the various occupied populations quickly found themselves suffering harsher and more brutal treatment than they had ever experienced under their former colonial rulers.

Hushed history

Japan's part in World War II – and its 20 million citizens killed – is still kept under wraps to a certain degree. Imperial Army documents are gradually being published, and veterans are starting to tell their stories, but in schools the role played in the atrocities by the Japanese is still played down.

The Battle of Midway, in June 1942 – destroying Japan's four aircraft carriers and soon thereafter its merchant navy and remaining naval air-power – cut Japan off from its empire. In 1944 General Douglas MacArthur was back in the Philippines to direct the island-hopping advance that ended in the massive fire-bombing of Japan's mostly wood-built cities. In an air raid by 130 B29s, Tokyo was devastated

One of the few structures to survive the blast
on 6 August 1945: the A-Bomb Dome in Hiroshima

and 100,000 of its inhabitants perished. But Japan was reluctant to sue for peace because the Allies were demanding unconditional surrender with no provision for maintaining the highly symbolic role of the emperor, still considered the embodiment of Japan's spirit and divine origins.

Despite US intelligence reports and monitored communications indicating the desperation of large sections of the Japanese government for peace, the Japanese rejection of the Potsdam Declaration calling for Japan's unconditional surrender was the excuse for unleashing the ultimate weapon of the war. On 6 August 1945, a B29 (the *Enola Gay*) dropped an atomic bomb on the city of Hiroshima, inflicting a level of destruction that astonished even the bomb's designers. Three days later another atomic bomb devastated the southern port of Nagasaki.

On 8 August the Soviet Union entered the Pacific battlefront and on the next day marched into Manchuria. Five days later the Japanese people heard the voice of Emperor Hirohito, in his first radio

Statue of a Japanese
World War II pilot

broadcast, announcing that 'the war situation has developed not necessarily to Japan's advantage'. The emperor renounced his divinity, and US forces took formal control of Japan.

Peace and Prosperity

Despite an alarming rise in prostitution, a high incidence of rape of Japanese women by US personnel, double standards for legal redress and strict censorship (reports and images of the atomic bombings, for example, were not permitted to be published), the occupation years were not as dire as most Japanese citizens had been led to believe by years of wartime government propaganda. The postwar period began, however, with millions of displaced people homeless and starving. To counter a perceived communist threat from the Soviet Union, the US quickly set to work reconstructing the economy by transforming Japan's institutions and devising a new pacifist constitution. Article 9 renounced Japan's right to maintain armed forces, although the ambiguous wording was later taken to permit the creation of a 'self-defence' force.

The *zaibatsu* conglomerates that had proved so instrumental in boosting Japan's militarism were disbanded, later to re-emerge as the *keiretsu* trading conglomerates that dominated the economy once again. The entire economy received a massive jump-start with the outbreak of the Korean War, with Japan ironically becoming the chief local supplier for an army it had battled against so furiously just a few years earlier.

The occupation lasted until 1952, having already planted the seeds for Japan's future stunning economic success. Economic output was back to prewar levels, and British auto companies provided the support needed to get Japan's motor industry back on its feet. Japanese companies then enthusiastically imported any Western technologies they could get their hands on. This included transistor technology – invented in the US but then considered to have only limited applications – for the surreal sum of $25,000. It was Japan that produced the world's first transistor radio. The electronic technology spurt that followed is now legendary.

Parliamentary democracy finally came into its own, albeit with distinctly Japanese characteristics reflecting the dislike of debate and confrontation and the group-oriented preference for maintaining the appearance of harmony at all times. The government, through the powerful Finance Ministry and Ministry of International Trade and Industry, generously supported favoured private corporations: first shipping, then cars, then electronics firms basked in the warmth of the government's loving attentions.

Economic prosperity has transformed Tokyo

Japan overtook Britain economically in 1964. By the end of the decade, Japan's was the third largest economy in the world – less then two decades after the war had left the country in ruins. Unusually, for a developing or developed country, Japan's new national wealth was evenly distributed among the people, leaving almost no one in an economic lower class. Unemployment remained low. Industrial labour disputes and strikes were minimal. Prosperity was not without its own problems, however: pollution caused by 'dirty' industries; a high incidence of stomach ulcers (even suicides) among school-children pressured by over-ambitious parents; and the awkward questions of what to do about nuclear energy.

The famous cosiness among politicians, bureaucrats and private companies, together with the strong cultural emphasis on rela-tionship-building and a lack of transparency and accountability, eventually led to corrupt practices of endemic proportions. Breach-of-trust scandals became common. In an increasingly producer-led economy dominated by price-fixing cartels operating with the gov-ernment's blessing, consumers were left to foot the bill.

The Inevitable Collapse

The start of asset inflation in the 1980s led to the 'bubble econ-omy', with anyone owning land becoming richer by the minute. At one point the land value of the Imperial Palace in Tokyo was thought to be worth more than the entire real-estate value of Cana-da. With astonishing sums of money sloshing around the econo-my and Japanese products considered world-beaters everywhere, it seemed to the Japanese that the nation had finally achieved its rightful place in the world.

Everyone expected the double-digit growth rates to continue in-definitely. However, crashing property prices had a domino effect on the rest of the economy, and in the early 1990s Japan slipped quickly into stagnation and then recession. Seemingly endemic cor-ruption was compounded by a remarkable dearth of political lead-ership and decisive action. Indeed, in Japan's consensus-based management system, the response of politicians, bureaucrats, and business leaders seemed to be to look the other way and hope bad news would disappear.

The government's gradual and reluctant admission that, despite previous assurances, banks were sitting on staggering – and long-concealed – amounts of unrecoverable loans (originally secured against land values) caused an unprecedented crisis of confidence.

Growing economic decline brought record corporate bankruptcies and the end of lifetime employment, as companies were forced to improve efficiency in order to survive.

The irony is that although Japan has continually triumphed over externally imposed adversity and upheavals, it seems unable to implement effective reforms to its own systems before problems reach crisis proportions. The rote-learning educational system is still failing to help students develop the individual analytical and problem-solving skills required in the information age. Another example is the banking crisis, which grew to globally alarming proportions over an eight-year period before the government even admitted a problem existed.

Despite these formidable challenges, Japan will probably end up confounding the pessimists. It will most likely emerge in the 21st century as a regional leader in more than just economic terms. No matter what the future holds, Japan will remain one of the world's most intriguing destinations for travellers everywhere.

The futuristic Tokyo Metropolitan Government Office building

Historical Landmarks

Jomon Culture (c.10,000–300BC)
660BC Legendary founding of first imperial dynasty.

Yayoi Culture (c.300BC–AD300)
Wheel-made pottery and wet rice cultivation arrive from China and Korea.

Kofun Period (c.300–710)
c.300 Unification of Japan under Yamato Court. Period of Chinese influence.
c.538 Introduction of Buddhism from China. Rise to power of Soga family.
645 Soga ousted by Nakatomi Kamatari, founder of Fujiwara dynasty.

Nara Period (710–784)
710 Imperial Court established at Nara.

Heian Period (794–1185)
794 Imperial Court moves to Heian-kyo.
1156 Four-year war between Taira and Minamoto clans.

Kamakura Period (1192–1333)
1192 Yoritomo Minamoto becomes first shogun.
1274–81 Unsuccessful Mongol invasions under Kublai Khan.
1333 Fall of Kamakura.

Muromachi Period (1338–1573)
1339–1573 Shogunate of Ashikaga family.
1467–1568 Civil war between provincial daimyo (Age of Warring States).
1543–49 Arrival of Portuguese explorers and Jesuit missionaries.
1568 Rise to power of Nobunaga, Hideyoshi and Tokugawa.

Momoyama Period (1573–1600)
1582 Nobunaga assassinated; Hideyoshi succeeds him.
1592 Hideyoshi launches failed attack on Korea and China.
1598 Death of Hideyoshi; Tokugawa seizes power.

Edo Period (1603–1867)

1603 Tokugawa Ieyasu takes title of shogun; capital established at Edo (Tokyo).

1635 Isolation of Japan from rest of world begins.

1854 Treaty of Kanagawa opens Japan to US trade.

Meiji Restoration (1868–1912)

1868 Emperor Meiji comes to throne.

1894–95 Sino-Japanese War.

1904–5 Russo-Japanese War.

Modern Period (1912–present)

1937 Japan declares war on Chinese Nationalists.

1940 Japan joins Axis powers in World War II.

1941 Japan bombs Pearl Harbor.

1945 Atom bombs are dropped on Hiroshima (6 August) and Nagasaki (9 August); Japan surrenders.

1945–52 US occupation of Japan.

1964 Tokyo hosts the Olympic Games: a turning point in its economy, marking Japan's re-entry into the international community.

1952–93 Rapid growth and industrialisation make Japan the world's second-richest nation.

1970 World-famous author Yukio Mishima commits ritual suicide after a failed coup calling for the restoration of the Emperor.

1989 Death of Emperor Hirohito; Akihito succeeds to throne.

1993–2009 Japan enters and continues to be in prolonged slowdown, with little sign of the much promised restructuring of its economy.

1995 An earthquake hits the Kobe area, killing over 6,000 people and leaving 300,000 homeless. Death cult Aum Shinrikyo unleash sarin gas in the Tokyo subway system, killing 12 and injuring hundreds.

2001 Birth of first child of Crown Prince Naruhito and Crown Princess Masako starts debate over male-only succession law.

2003 Japan sends members of its self-defence force to Iraq.

2008 Massive, successful protest by Okinawans against the plan to remove references to the military's role in the forced suicides of Okinawan civilians.

WHERE TO GO

To help you plan your itinerary, we divide Japan into seven regional sections. The first is devoted entirely to Tokyo, where you're likely to begin your trip, get your bearings and become acquainted with modern Japan. We then present six tours spreading out from the capital to the centres of historic and artistic interest as well as to sites of natural beauty. If you have sufficient time to explore Japan, you might want to begin and end your visit in Tokyo. In between, you can venture out to explore the rest of the country.

TOKYO

Originally known as Edo (meaning 'mouth of the estuary'), **Tokyo** was just a sleepy little village surrounded by marshland on the broad Kanto plain until the end of the 16th century, when Tokugawa Ieyasu moved here and made it the centre of his vast domains. When Ieyasu became shogun in 1603, Edo in turn became the seat of national government – and its castle the largest in the world. Edo expanded rapidly to accommodate Ieyasu's 80,000 retainers and their families and the myriad common people who served their daily needs. By 1787 the population had grown to 1,368,000.

The ruling élite lived on the high ground, the Yamanote ('bluffs') west and south of the castle. The artisans, tradespeople and providers of entertainment (reputable and not so reputable) lived 'downtown' on

> **Metropolis**
>
> In the 17th century, Tokyo was the largest city in the world, with over a million inhabitants. Soon after World War I the city's population grew to 3 million, then crossed the 9-million mark in the 1970s.

the reclaimed marshlands north and east, in the area that is still known as Shitamachi. As these two populations interacted, a unique new culture was born. Edo became the centre of power and

Tokyo, city of neon lights and giant screens

also the centre of all that was vibrant and compelling in the arts.

After 1868 that centre grew even stronger, when the movement known as the Meiji Restoration overthrew the Tokugawa shogunate and the imperial court moved to Edo. The city was renamed Tokyo ('Eastern Capital'), and from that moment on all roads – political, cultural and financial – led here.

In the 20th century Tokyo twice suffered almost total destruction. First, the earthquake of 1923 and subsequent fire razed nearly all vestiges of old Edo, killing some 140,000 people in the process. Rebuilt without any comprehensive urban plan, Tokyo remains a city of subcentres and neighbourhoods, even villages, each with its own distinct personality.

Unlike the great capital cities of Europe, there is no prevailing style of architecture here, no 'monumental' core for a new building to harmonise with. Even after the collapse of the economic bubble, construction projects are everywhere. Whole blocks of the city seem to disappear overnight, replaced in the blink of an eye by new office buildings, cultural complexes and shopping centres.

Tokyo is a city of enormous creative and entrepreneurial energy, much of which goes into reinventing itself. If there's a commodity in short supply here, it's relaxation. Nobody 'strolls' in Tokyo, and there are few places to sit down outdoors and watch the world go by. The idea of a long, leisurely lunch hour is utterly alien. People in Tokyo are in a hurry to get somewhere – even if they don't always know precisely where they're going.

The Imperial Palace

If Tokyo can be said to have any centre at all, this is it. Today's **Imperial Palace** is on the site of Edo castle, where the Tokugawa shogunate ruled Japan for 265 years; it was thereafter home to the emperors of the modern era. The palace was almost totally destroyed in the air raids of World War II, then rebuilt in ferroconcrete. This is the least interesting part of what was once the largest system of fortifications in the world, and in any case you can't get in to see it. What you can see are the lovely grounds of the East Garden, the moat and massive stone ramparts, and those few examples of classic Japanese architecture – gates, bridges, armouries and watchtowers – that have survived since the 17th century.

The imperial family still resides in the palace, so the general public is admitted to the grounds on only two days each year: on 2 January and 23 December. On these occasions, you might find it hard to compete with the many thousands of Japanese visitors who come to pay their respects.

To reach the Imperial Palace's **East Garden** (Tue–Thur and Sat–Sun 9am–4pm, Nov–Feb until 3.30pm), from Otemachi subway station, enter the gardens at the Otemon Gate and wander along hedgerows of white and pink azaleas, around ponds and little waterfalls edged with pines, plum trees, canary palms and soft green *Cryptomeria japonica*. Over the treetops you catch an occasional glimpse of the skyscrapers of modern Tokyo. North of the garden, but still enclosed within the palace moat, the densely wooded Kitanomaru Park contains the redbrick **Craft Gallery** (Tue–Sun 10am–5pm). The gallery, housed in a Meiji-era building, is a first-rate

introduction to Japanese arts and crafts. Also within the park is a **Science Museum** (Tue–Sun 9am–4.30pm), with interactive displays and hi-tech exhibits, and the distinctive **Nippon Budokan**, a martial arts hall.

A walk clockwise around the palace grounds will bring you first to the picturesque **Nijubashi Bridge** and the Seimon Gate, where the public is allowed to enter the palace grounds. You then pass the most prominent of Japan's modern government buildings, the **National Diet** (Japan's parliament) and the **Supreme Court**. A complete circuit would also include the **National Theatre** and the **National Museum of Modern Art** (Tue–Sun 10am–5pm, Fri until 8pm; www.momat.go.jp). With a short detour, you can also take

The Imperial Palace grounds are visible from Niju-bashi bridge

in **Yasukuni Jinja**. Founded in 1869, this is the 'Shrine of Peace for the Nation', dedicated to the souls of those who have died for Japan in battle. Besides the main hall and the hall of worship, the shrine complex includes a *noh* theatre stage, a *sumo* wrestling ring, several teahouses and the Yushukan museum of war memorabilia (daily 9am–5pm). A spacious addition to the museum, an all-glass building, contains several new exhibits, including a Zero fighter plane.

Ginza

Tokyo's best-known district is named after a silver mint originally located here. After a period of losing out to newer, fresher fashion zones like Minami-Aoyama and Daikanyama, the **Ginza**, with new stores like Gucci, Chanel and the extraordinary Ginza Mikimoto 2 in place, is once again the acme of Tokyo chic.

The windows of such department stores as Wako and Mitsukoshi are works of art. Inside, there's more art: all the major department stores project themselves as bastions of culture, maintaining their own galleries and mounting frequent world-class exhibitions of prints, painting, pottery and sculpture. Downstairs you can find still more 'art' – to Western eyes at least – in the astonishing basement gourmet food displays. (The basement is also a good place for cheaper snacks than you'll find in the street-level restaurants.)

North of the main Ginza 4-chome crossing is **Hibiya Koen**, Tokyo's first Western-style park, and the futuristic **Tokyo Inter-**

national Forum, an architectural bombshell made almost entirely of glass. It contains concert halls, restaurants and a sweeping atrium called the Glass Hall.

Running roughly north–south through Ginza from the corner of Hibiya Park all the way to Tokyo Bay is the broad avenue called Harumi-dori. Taking a stroll down the avenue is such a national pastime that there's even a colloquial expression for it: *gin-bura*. Just south of Ginza itself, as you walk towards the bay, you see on your left the red lanterns and long banners of the **Kabuki-za**, home base for that most thrilling and colourful form of traditional Japanese drama. The first kabuki theatre was built in on this site in 1889. Designed to invoke the castle architecture of the Tokugawa period, the theatre was destroyed in an air raid in World War II and rebuilt in 1949.

Still further south is the **Tsukiji Central Wholesale Market** (Mon–Sat, shops close around 1pm) – one of the largest fish markets in the world. Some 1,600 wholesale dealers do business here, supplying 90 percent of the fish consumed in Tokyo every day. Sadly the tuna auctions are no longer open to the public, but still get here early (7am is ideal) and enjoy the orchestrated pandemonium of the market at its finest. From here, you could walk to the Hama Rikyu **Detached Palace Garden**. Originally a Tokugawa family estate, the garden became a public park in 1945. The path to the left as you enter leads to the ferry landing, where the 'river buses' depart for their journeys up the Sumida River to Asakusa.

Asakusa

Asakusa is the heart of Shitamachi, the quarter best-beloved of that fractious, gossipy, prodigal population called the Edokko, who trace their 'downtown' roots back at least three generations. Edokko are suckers for sentimentality and for *ninjo*: the web of small favours and kindnesses that bind them together. Sneeze in the night and your Edokko neighbour will demand the next morning that you take better care of yourself; stay at home with a temperature, and he or she will be over by noon with a bowl of soup. An Edokko craftsman

Other Tokyo Museums

Idemitsu Museum of Arts (Tue–Sun 10am–5pm, Fri until 7pm; www.idemitsu.co.jp; Yuraku-cho Station, JR Yamanote line). A major collection of Chinese porcelain of the Tang and Song dynasties, and Japanese ceramics in all the classic styles. There are also outstanding examples of Zen painting and calligraphy, wood-block prints and paintings of the Edo period.

Edo-Tokyo Museum (Tue–Sun 9.30am–5.30pm, Sat until 7.30pm; www.edo-tokyo-museum.or.jp; Ryogoku station, Hanzomon subway, JR Sobu line). The best museum chronicling the history of Tokyo features a reconstructed Nihonbashi Bridge, a life size model of a kabuki stage, scale models of Tokyo districts and wealthy residences as they once were, displays on woodblock printing, and photos showing the destruction caused by the air raids of World War II. The museum is housed in a futuristic building.

Japanese Sword Museum (Tue–Sun 9am–4.30pm; Sangubashi Station, Odakyu line from Shinjuku). A splendid introduction to the noble and lethal history of Japanese swords – the closest that weapons have ever come to being great works of art.

Mingeikan: Japan Folk Arts Museum (Tue–Sun 10am–5pm; www.mingeikan.or.jp; Komaba Todai-mae Station, Keio-Inokashira line from Shibuya). Home to excellent examples of ceramics, lacquerware, woodcraft and textiles. It gives a particularly good insight into Japanese furniture that you might not obtain in a private home.

Nezu Institute of Fine Arts (closed for renovation, garden remains open; www.nezu-muse.or.jp; Omotesando Station, Ginza line). Outstanding works of Japanese painting, calligraphy and ceramics – including some designated as National Treasures. Finer yet, perhaps, is the Institute's wonderful garden: an exquisite composition of pines and flowering shrubs, ponds and waterfalls, moss-covered stone lanterns and tea pavilions.

would rather lose a commission than take any guff from a customer who doesn't know good work when he sees it. Edokko quarrel in a language all their own. Ignore the proprieties – or offend the pride of an Edokko – and he will let you know about it, in no uncertain terms; respect his sense of values and you make a friend for life.

The heart of Asakusa is **Sensoji** (also known as the **Asakusa Kannon temple**). According to legend, the temple houses a small statue of the Buddhist goddess of mercy, found in the Sumida River by two local fishermen in the year 628 – but in fact not even the temple priests have ever seen it. When Edo became the capital of the Tokugawa shogunate, Asakusa began to flourish as an entertainment quarter. In the early 19th century even the kabuki theatres were located here. The Meiji Restoration and the opening of Japan to exotic new Western-style amusements further enhanced Asakusa's reputation as Fun City. The Kamiya Bar, the city's first Western-style watering hole, opened in 1880 (and is still doing business);

'Bathing' in the smoke of the Sensoji incense burner is believed to bestow a year's good luck

the first cinema opened here in 1903. Before long, the streets and alleys around the temple were filled with music halls, burlesque theatres, cabarets, gambling dens and watering holes of every type.

Take a cruise

The Asakusa's Azuma Bridge pier is a good place to board *suijo-basu* (waterbuses) for a cruise: Tokyo Water Cruise, tel: (03) 5733-4812, www.suijo bus.co.jp/english/index.

Most of the temple quarter was firebombed to ashes in 1945, but by 1958 the people of the area had raised enough money to rebuild Sensoji and all of the important structures around it. So what if the restorations were in concrete? The original is still there in spirit – and no visitor should neglect it.

Sensoji Temple and Surroundings

Start your exploration from Asakusa Station, on the Ginza subway line (Tokyo's first subway). A few steps from the exit is **Kaminarimon** ('**Thunder God Gate**'), the main entrance to the temple, hung with a pair of enormous red paper lanterns. From here, the long, narrow arcade called Nakamise-dori is lined with shops selling toasted rice crackers, spices in gourd-shaped wooden bottles, dolls, toys, fans, children's kimono and ornaments and souvenirs of all sorts. Some of these shops have been operated by the same families for hundreds of years.

The arcade ends at a two-storey gate called the Hozomon. To the left is the Five-Storey Pagoda, and across the courtyard is the main hall of Sensoji. Visitors should be sure to stop at the huge bronze incense burner in front of the hall, to 'bathe' in the smoke – an observance believed to bestow a year's worth of good health.

The building to the right of the main hall is the **Asakusa Jinja**, a Shinto shrine dedicated to the three legendary founders – the Sanja – of Sensoji. (Buddhism and Shinto get along quite peacefully in Japan, sharing ground and even deities.) The Sanja Matsuri, held here every year on the third weekend in May, is the biggest, most exuberant festival in Tokyo.

This *tatami*-mat room is part of a full-scale reproduction of an Edo-period house in the Shitamachi Museum

Ueno

North of the city centre, **Ueno** was chosen in 1625 by the Tokugawa Shogun Hidetaka as the site of a vast temple complex. Called **Kan'eiji**, it was established on the area's one prominent hill to protect the capital from evil spirits. Kan'eiji was a seat of great power until 1868, when it became the battleground in the shogunate's last stand against the imperial army and most of the buildings were destroyed. Subsequently, Ueno was turned into Tokyo's first public park, endowed with all the preferred Western improvements: museums, concert halls, a library, a university of fine arts and a zoo. Ueno should be a stop on any visitor's itinerary – especially if you happen to be here in mid-April, when the cherry blossoms in the park are glorious.

No visitor here should miss the **Tokyo National Museum** (Tue–Sun 9.30am–5pm, Apr–Dec Sat–Sun until 6pm), a complex of five buildings devoted to Japanese art and archaeology dating back to the prehistoric Jomon and Yayoi periods. Outstanding among the exhibits are Buddhist sculpture of the 10th- and 11th-century Heian era, illustrated narrative scrolls from the 13th-century Kamakura period, paintings by the great Muromachi artist Sesshu and woodblock prints by the Edo-period masters Utamaro, Hiroshige and Hokusai. Nor should you neglect the **National Museum of Western Art** (Tue–Sun 9.30am–5.30pm, Fri until 8pm), on the east side of Ueno Park: an outstanding collection of French Impressionist paintings, prints and drawings, the gift of a wealthy businessman named Kojiro Matsukata. The building itself was designed by Le Corbusier; the Rodin sculptures in the courtyard – the *Gate of Hell,* the *Thinker* and the magnificent *Burghers of Calais* – are authentic castings from the original moulds.

Of the Edo-era buildings that have survived or been restored, the most important are the main hall of Kan'eiji and the **Toshogu Shrine** to the first Tokugawa Shogun Ieyasu – a lesser version of the great sanctum at Nikko, in the mountains of Nagano Prefecture *(see page 66)*. Also of interest is the **Kiyomizu Kannon Hall**, modelled after the larger and more famous Kiyomizu temple in Kyoto; registered as a National Treasure, this is one of the few buildings that survived the battle of 1868 intact.

At the south end of the park is the statue of Saigo Takamori, leader of the imperial army that overthrew the shogunate in 1868. (Saigo is a problematic hero in Japanese history: in 1871 he was killed in an unsuccessful rebellion against the very government he helped to found.)

From here, it's a short walk west to the grounds of **Shinobazu Pond**, with its lotuses and water fowl. Just inside the entrance, on the right, is the **Shitamachi Museum** (Tue–Sun 9.30am–4.30pm). Spend some time here: it will give

Shinobazu

A shortage of land has seen Shinobazu used for several purposes, including as a horse-racing track in the Meiji era and for growing vegetables during the war. Mercifully, a plan a few years ago to build a car park beneath the pond was dropped after locals opposed the scheme.

you a wonderfully concrete sense of the lifestyle that defined this part of the city for well over 300 years. The displays include a full-scale reproduction of a *nagaya* (one of the long, single-storey terraced houses typical of the Edo period). Visitors are welcome to take their shoes off and walk through the *tatami*-mat rooms.

North of Ueno is **Yanaka**, one of Tokyo's best preserved older quarters. A traditional temple area of back alleys, graced with wooden houses, public baths, private galleries and craft shops, Yanaka Cemetery is a time-capsule of mossy tombs, leafy paths and weathered Buddhist statuary.

Harajuku and Yoyogi Park

The venerable imperial traditions of Japan and the frenetic celebration of its youth culture are arrayed side by side in this quarter of the city. From Harajuku Station on the Japan Railways Yamanote loop line, it's but a few steps to **Meiji Jingu**, the shrine dedicated to the spirits of the Emperor Meiji (who died in 1912) and the Empress Shoken. The entrance is marked by two huge *torii* gates, their pillars made from 1,700-year-old cypress trees.

From here, broad gravel paths lead to the *honden* (the sanctum of the shrine), destroyed in the air raids of 1945 and restored in 1958, and the **Imperial Treasure House Museum** (Sat–Sun 9am–4.30pm). The Meiji emperor presided over the emergence of Japan as a modern nation state, and his shrine is surely the most solemn, decorous place in Tokyo. During the annual festival (3 November) and on New Year's Day, as many as a million people will come to offer prayers and pay their respects. Spring and summer make better visits, when you can admire the irises and flowering shrubs of the inner gardens.

Adjacent to the shrine is **Yoyogi Park**. The park is remarkable chiefly for the National Yoyogi Sports Centre, comprising two stadiums designed by architect Tange Kenzo. The park itself was once a parade ground for the imperial Japanese army.

A couple at the shrine at Meiji-jingu

After World War II it was taken over by the Occupation for military housing and nicknamed 'Washington Heights', then redeveloped as the Olympic Village site for the 1964 Tokyo Olympic Games. By the 1980s, thanks to the broad avenues and new subway stops built for the games, this had become one of the liveliest, trendiest and demographically youngest quarters of the city. Street food, body paint, in-your-face fashion, photo ops: on a warm spring afternoon Yoyogi Park is more fun than any other place in town.

Takeshita-dori, just across the railway bridge from the park, continues this spirit of avant-garde fashion with gangs like the cosplay-zoku, groups of mostly female youngsters in manga-inspired costumes and lemon and blue lipstick, turning the narrow street into a lively and impromptu catwalk of the new and bizarre.

The south end of the park borders on Shibuya, where you can visit **NHK Broadcasting Centre**, headquarters of Japan's public television network – a must for anyone wishing to see how samurai epics are made. Your hotel or the Tourist Information

An artist at work in Shinjuku
Gyoen National Garden

Centre will have information on the 'Studio Park' guided tour of the NHK soundstages.

Shinjuku

In the Edo period **Shinjuku** was where two of the major roads from the west came together. By the early 1900s the area had become a sort of bohemian quarter, beloved of the city's cliques of writers, artists and intellectuals. After World War II it emerged as one of Tokyo's major transportation hubs, and today an estimated three million people pass through Shinjuku Station every day. The station itself divides Shinjuku into two distinctly different areas, east and west.

West Shinjuku rejoices in a special gift of nature. Its relatively stable bedrock can support earthquake-safe skyscrapers – foremost among them is the Metropolitan Government Office, more familiarly known as **Tokyo City Hall**. The City Hall complex was architect Tange Kenzo's magnum opus, arguably the last great work of his career. The complex, completed in 1991, consists of a 48-storey main office building, a 34-storey annexe, the Metropolitan Assembly building and a huge central courtyard. The main building soars 243m (799ft), splitting on the 33rd floor into two towers. Weather permitting, the observation decks on the 45th floors of both towers offer views all the way to Mt Fuji (north observatory: Tue–Sun 9am–1pm, south observatory: Wed–Mon 9.30am–5pm).

South of the City Hall, across busy Koshu kaido Avenue, the **Bunka Gakuen Costume Museum** (Mon–Sat 10am–4.30pm), has a fabulous collection of clothing, dating from the Heian and Edo periods, right up to the fashions of the 1960s. West of the museum, the massive **Tokyo Opera City** is a business, shopping and cultural complex that includes the New National Theatre and an excellent multi-media art space called the **NTT InterCommunication Centre** (Tue–Sun 10am–6pm) with interactive displays and innovative high-tech exhibits.

East Shinjuku is really two places: a daytime quarter of department stores, vertical malls and discount stores, and a night-time quarter of bars (straight and gay), cheap restaurants, strip joints, game parlours, jazz clubs, rooms-by-the-hour hotels, raves and honky-tonks – most of the latter in a seedy, neon-lit neighbourhood called **Kabuki-cho**. The neighbourhood isn't really dangerous, but it's all too easy for the unwary visitor to wander

Little Buds, Big Obsession

Nightly news bulletins track the progress of the 'front' moving across the country at some time in April or May. Anticipation reaches fever pitch as people everywhere prepare to make pilgrimages to favourite vantage points across the country. It's cherry blossom season once again.

The tradition of formal blossom appreciation and viewing goes back centuries. In Kyoto and Nara, for instance, special viewing pavilions were built for the aristocracy specifically for this purpose. Today, Maruyama Park in Kyoto's Gion district is where numerous drinking parties are held under the blossoms in a cathartic mass-shedding of the usual Japanese reserve. And the grounds of the Osaka Mint heave with citizens trying to catch a glimpse of what is reputedly among the finest examples of the nation's most cherished and celebrated asset.

Over 150 varieties exist, varying in terms of size, colour and exact blooming time. Why the big fuss over these precious pink petals? For many Japanese, the cherry blossom epitomises the fleeting nature of beauty and purity, the concepts of transience and impermanence that imbue so many aspects of Japanese culture, psyche and even identity. During World War II, Japan's notorious kamikaze suicide pilots were even romanticised as human cherry blossoms, their young lives abruptly ending after a supposedly dazzling moment of glory.

into a rip-off; if you plan to explore Kabuki-cho, do so with a knowledgeable local guide.

A longish walk along Shinjuku-dori from the station will bring you to the north end of **Shinjuku Gyoen National Garden**. This collection of gardens (in Japanese, French and English styles) became part of the imperial household after the Meiji Restoration and, in 1949, a public park – the ultimate oasis in this quarter of the city. Shinjuku Gyoen is famous for its botanical greenhouse, for its flowering cherry trees in April and for its chrysanthemum exhibition during the first two weeks of October.

Still on the east side of the railway tracks, a short stroll west of the gardens is **Takashimaya Times Square**. An enthralling complex of stores, a virtual reality arcade, cafés, restaurants and theatres, this is Shinjuku's latest addition to innovative shopping and entertainment.

Shinagawa and Odaiba

Not otherwise rich in tourist attractions, Shinagawa has one gem that should not be missed: **Sengakuji**, the temple where 47 *ronin*, or masterless samurai, brought the head of Lord Kira, in a true life revenge story that has been told in countless kabuki plays, puppet dramas, films and TV dramas. The graves of the *ronin*, who were ordered to commit ritual suicide after exacting their revenge, are clearly marked, and those who still honour them come to burn incense at their tombs. The graves of their slain master, Lord Asano, and his wife are also here. The small Museum of the Loyal Retainers contains weapons, personal effects and memorabilia.

The highlight of the Tokyo bay area is **Odaiba**, a man-made island and experimental architectural zone connected to the mainland by a driverless train, the Yurikamome line. Stops along the line take in the graceful **Rainbow Bridge**, Kenzo Tange's **Fuji TV** building, the **National Museum of Emerging Science and Innovation**, the surreal Venus Fort shopping mall, and the extraordinary **Tokyo Big Sight**, an exhibition centre in the form of two massive inverted pyramids.

KANTO

The once-marshy plain of **Kanto** is Tokyo's hinterland, the region where the feudal warlords set up their military bases and administrative headquarters. Their tough-minded pragmatism survives today not only in Tokyo but also in the dynamic industrial zone that has burgeoned around it in such towns as Kawasaki and Yokohama. The Kanto area is vital to Japan's economy, producing nearly a third of the country's entire domestic gross product. But monuments at Kamakura and Nikko still bear testimony to the region's history. And reigning supreme over Kanto is a sublime spiritual comment on the vanity of all such human endeavours: sacred Mt Fuji.

Four easy-to-manage excursions from Tokyo would make memorable additions to your stay. Two of them – to Yokohama and Kamakura – are daytrips. Visits to Nikko and to Mt Fuji/ Hakone will be more enjoyable as overnighters.

The volcanic landscapes of Kanto – Tokyo's hinterland

Nikko

'Think nothing splendid', says an old Japanese proverb, 'until you've seen Nikko'. In the mountains of Tochigi Prefecture, about 150km (93 miles) north of Tokyo by train, **Nikko** (www.nikko-jp. org) is the final resting place of Ieyasu, founder of the Tokugawa shogunate, who died in 1616. Upon his death he was declared a god by the imperial court and subsequently known as Tosho Daigongen ('The Great Incarnation Who Illuminates the East'). The following year, his remains were taken in a grand procession to be enshrined here, on the site of a religious centre founded some eight centuries before. In life, Ieyasu had made himself the absolute monarch of Japan. His personal fief alone was worth enough to feed and support some 2.5 million people. **Toshogu**, (Apr–Oct 8am–5pm, Nov–Mar 8am–4pm) the mausoleum complex that he commanded for himself in his apotheosis, is extraordinary.

Nikko is best reached from Tokyo by train (by the Japan Railways Shinkansen line from Tokyo or Ueno stations, with a transfer at Utsunomiya, or by the private Tobu Line 'Limited Express' from Asakusa). The journey takes about two hours. The little town of Nikko is essentially one long avenue from the railway station to the Toshogu shrine.

The Toshogu Shrine Complex

A short bus ride from the station plaza brings you to the recently renovated red-lacquer **Shinkyo** ('Sacred Bridge'), a 28m (92ft) span over the Daiya River, where your exploration of Toshogu begins. The bridge marks the spot where the Buddhist priest Shodo is said to have crossed the river in the year 766 on the backs of two huge serpents to found the temple that would later become Rinnoji. An entrance to the shrine complex is just across the road, opposite the bridge and up a flight of stone steps that brings you first to Shodo's temple.

Rinnoji belongs to the Tendai sect of Buddhism. The main hall, called the Sanbutsudo, with its almost erotic colour scheme of black and green and vermilion, dates to 1648 and is the largest single building at Toshogu. Inside are three huge gold-lacquered

The sanctuary at Toshogu

states, all measuring 8m (26ft) in height, representing three different manifestations of the Buddha. In the centre is Amida Nyorai, the Buddha who leads believers to Paradise; on the right is Senju ('Thousand-Armed') Kannon, the goddess of mercy; on the left is Bato-Kannon, depicted with a horse's head on its forehead, regarded as the protector of animals. North of the main hall is the Goho-tendo, a subtemple where worshippers inscribe their prayers for health and prosperity on slats of wood that are later burned to carry the prayers to heaven. To the south is the residence of the Abbot – by tradition an imperial prince – with a particularly fine garden in the style of the Edo period.

Leaving Rinnoji from the west side, you come to the broad Omote-sando avenue that leads uphill to the shrine itself. Note the monument to the daimyo Matsudaira Masatane, Ieyasu's trusted retainer. Matsudaira spent some 20 years planting the majestic cryptomeria cedars on the grounds of the shrine and along the 64km (40 mile) avenue of approach. Alas, much of the avenue has been destroyed; a few sections of it survive on the road east of town, where many of the 13,000 trees still standing are maintained by corporate sponsors.

At the top of the Omote-sando, on the left, is the five-storey pagoda of the shrine, decorated with the 12 signs of the Asian zodiac and the hollyhock crest of the Tokugawa family. From here, a flight of stone steps leads to the first gate of Toshogu: the Omote-mon, guarded by two fierce red-painted Deva kings. In the first courtyard is the stable, which houses the shrine's sacred white horse; the carved panel above the door is the famous group of three monkeys – 'Hear no evil, see no evil, speak no evil!' – that has become a symbol of Nikko, the logo on virtually every souvenir. At the far end of the courtyard is the Kyozo (Sutra Library), which houses an estimated 7,000 Buddhist scriptures in a huge revolving bookcase (not open to the public).

As you approach a second set of stone steps, you see on the right a belfry and a tall bronze candelabrum; on the left is a drum tower and a bronze revolving lantern. The two bronzes were presented

The sculpted, gilded roof of one of the many temples at Nikko

in the mid-17th century by the Dutch government, in gratitude for the special exemption that gave its merchants exclusive trading privileges with Japan during the period of national seclusion. Off to the left is the Yakushi-do, a temple honouring the manifestation of the Buddha as healer of illnesses.

At the top of the steps is the two-storey **Yomeimon**, the 'Gate of Sunlight' – the triumphal masterpiece of Tosh-ogu, rightly declared a National Treasure. This is the ultimate expression of the opulent Momoyama style inspired by Chinese Ming sculpture and architecture. Ivory-white and 11.3m (37ft) high, its columns, beams and cornices are carved with a menagerie of dragons, phoenixes, lions and tigers in a field of clouds, peonies, Chinese sages and angels, all gilded and painted in red, gold, blue and green. To the right and left of the gate there are panelled galleries, also carved and painted with motifs from nature: pine and plum trees, birds of the field and waterfowl.

Inside the gate to the left is the Mikoshi-gura, a storeroom for the portable shrines that grace the semi-annual Toshogu Festival processions (17–18 May and 17 October). To the right is the Kagu-raden, a hall where ceremonial dances are performed to honour the gods – and where, for a modest fee, couples can have Shinto wedding ceremonies performed, complete with flutes and drums and shrine maidens to attend them.

Opposite the Yomeimon, across the courtyard, is the **Karamon** ('Chinese Gate'), the official entrance to the inner shrine. This structure, like Yomeimon, is also classified as a National Treasure and just as ornately carved and painted. The walls on both sides of this gate enclose the *honden* (main hall) of the shrine. The en-

---

Foreign influences

Although very Japanese in feel, Nikko has been influenced by other nationalities. The main sanctuary features the statues of three Chinese figures, as well as sculptures of mandarins – fruit then otherwise unknown in Japan. Numerous architectural treasures at Nikko were produced by Koreans.

Visitors en route to Tokugawa Ieyasu's tomb

trance is to the right. Here you remove your shoes (lockers are provided) to visit the outer part of the hall, called the *haiden* (oratory). You may not proceed further than this, for at the far end of the oratory are the *nai-jin* (inner chamber) and *nai-nai-jin* (innermost chamber), where the spirit of Ieyasu is enshrined. With him are two other worthy companions: Toyotomi Hideyoshi, Ieyasu's mentor, and the great 12th-century warrior Minamoto no Yoritomo, who founded the Kamakura shogunate – and whom Ieyasu claimed as an ancestor.

The tour next takes you to another Toshogu icon: the famous **Gate of the Sleeping Cat**. The cat itself, on a small panel above the entrance, is said to have been sculpted by Hidari Jingoro, a legendary master carver of the Tokugawa period. From here a flight of 207 stone steps takes you up through a wonderful forest of cedars to **Tokugawa Ieyasu's tomb**, called Hoto. The climb is worth making, if only for the view, the trees and a cool, rushing stream. The tomb itself, a miniature bronze pagoda that houses the great shogun's ashes, is nothing special.

A short walk west from Toshogu itself is surely the oldest of the institutions on this holy ground. **Futarasan Jinja** (Apr–Oct 8am–5pm, Nov–Mar 9am–6pm) is a Shinto shrine founded in the 8th century to honour the deity Okuni-nushi-no-Mikoto ('God of the Ricefields'), his consort and their son. In one corner of the enclosure is the Ghost Lantern, a bronze lantern some 2.3m (7.5ft) high;

the deep nicks in the bronze were made by guards on duty at the shrine, who believed that the lantern transformed itself into a goblin at night. Such was the incredible cutting power of the Japanese sword – embellished perhaps a bit by Japanese superstition.

Iemitsu, who was Ieyasu's grandson and the third Tokugawa shogun (1603–51), undertook the building of Toshogu. He has his own resting place here at **Daiyu-in**, to the west of Futarasan. Smaller in scale, Daiyu-in is in fact the more impressive mausoleum, set on a forested hillside and approached by three flights of stone stairs and five decorative gates. The most impressive of these, at the top of the stairs, is the Yashamon ('She-Demon Gate'), so named for the figures in its four alcoves. The sanctum of the shrine, designated a National Treasure, has a gilded and lacquered altar some 3m (nearly 10ft) high, where a seated wooden figure of Iemitsu looks down upon his mighty works.

Meet-and-Greet Etiquette

Westernisation in Japan is much more than simply breathing new life into governmental and industrial practices. In daily life, for example, businessmen often shake hands not as an alternative but as a supplement to the good old-fashioned bow. The handshake seems to complement the respectful formality of a bow with something more satisfyingly personal and sincere, breaching the distance with distinctly un-Japanese physical contact.

Many visitors, though, are uncomfortable with the idea of bowing, since it has strong cultural associations with servility and inferiority. This is natural. But – like everything else in Japan – the significance of the bow needs to be taken in context. Bows are usually not given but exchanged. In a rigidly hierarchical society; the idea is mainly to convey mutual respect and only incidentally to acknowledge one's status relative to another. If you're still uncomfortable, think of it as a handshake using the entire body. When you meet most Japanese people, they'll be expecting to grip your hand. Even the most token bow you give will pleasantly surprise them.

Young woman in a kimono

Around Nikko

The waterfalls and forested hills of the **Nikko National Park** area are a welcome respite to the monumentality of Tokugawa architecture. Even if you are only here for a daytrip, you should take the 10km (6 mile) bus ride up the spectacular winding Irohazaka Highway to Chuzenji. Better yet, take a cab and stop at Akechi-daira, the halfway point. The view of Mt Nantai (2,484m/8,148ft) and the valley below is magnificent.

Lake Chuzenji, at 1,269m (4,163ft) above sea level, is the highest lake in Japan. It was made aeons ago when a now-dormant volcano erupted and blocked the river courses, creating two cataracts. The 97m (318ft) **Kegon-no-taki** at the south end is the country's most famous waterfall. A lift takes sightseers to an observation platform in the gorge below. The falls are most impressive after a summer rain, when the sunshine produces a single or even double rainbow in the spray. In the winter the falls form a spectacular cascade of icicles. At the gorge's north end, Ryuzu-no-taki ('Dragon's Head Falls') is broader but not as high; it has the additional merit of a teahouse, where you can sit and watch the falls.

Famous for its rainbow trout, Chuzenji is too cold for swimming most of the year, but visitors throng to this area for its spectacular spring and autumn scenery and for its numerous hot springs resorts. The most impressive historical monument on the eastern shore of the lake is Chuzenji, a subtemple of Toshogu's Rinnoji. The temple enshrines a 6m (19ft) standing figure of Kannon, the Goddess of Mercy, said to have been carved more than 1,000 years ago from the trunk of a single Judas tree.

Travellers with an interest in Japanese ceramics but little time to spare can combine a trip to Nikko with an excursion to **Mashiko**. Just 25km (15 miles) southeast of Nikko, this famous pottery town, with its shops, studios and street market is a good introduction to the more rustic forms of Japanese ceramic ware.

Yokohama

Situated 30km (19 miles) southwest of Tokyo, **Yokohama** was an unimportant little fishing village until 1854, when Japan's long centuries of self-imposed isolation came to an end. Foreign diplomats, traders and missionaries were at last able to enter the country. But the unrest they inspired prompted the Tokugawa government to move them all here, to a guarded compound on the village flats – ostensibly to guarantee their safety, but more importantly to contain the contamination of their uncouth ways and ideas.

The elegant *Nippon Maru* is docked in Yokohama harbour

The ploy worked well enough until the Meiji Restoration, when those Western ideas were needed to modernise the country. In 1859 Yokohama became an international port, and the burgeoning international community quickly spread beyond its confinement to the high ground still known today as the Bluff. In 1872 Japan's first railway went into service between Yokohama and Tokyo, and the city began to flourish.

The two cities have twice shared the same destructive

fate. The great Kanto earthquake of 1923 destroyed some 60,000 homes in Yokohama and took over 20,000 lives. The next 20 years of reconstruction and growth were wiped out overnight, in May 1945, when American bombers levelled nearly half the city. The harbour was hastily restored during the Korean War and today is one of the busiest and most important trading ports in the world.

With a population of some 3½ million, Yokohama no longer sits in Tokyo's shadow. In many respects, in fact, it is the more cosmopolitan city, preferred by many residents of the greater metropolitan area as a place to live and work. If you are on a short visit to Japan, your excursion time might be better spent elsewhere. But Yokohama's great waterfront, port redevelopment project, museums and restaurants should still keep it high on your list.

The Japan Railways Keihin-Tohoku line takes about 40 minutes from Tokyo to Sakuragi-cho Station in Yokohama; the faster *shinkansen* drops you off at Shin-Yokohama, on the outskirts of the city. From Sakuragi-cho it's a short walk to the waterfront (which is still referred to by its old name, the Bund) and to the South Pier and Yamashita Park. Here you can take a tour of the harbour on one of the sightseeing launches moored near the ship *Hikawa-maru*, now retired from service. It carried passengers between Yokohama and Seattle for some 30 years; in summer, it has a pleasant beer garden on the upper deck. At the entrance to the South Pier is the nine-storey Silk Centre Building. The **Silk Museum** (Tue–Sun 9am–4.30pm; www.silkmuseum.or.jp) on the second floor, with its collection of kimono and exhibits of the silk-making process, evokes the period when Yokohama was the hub of that industry. Next door you will find an office of the Yokohama Convention and Visitors' Bureau. For a bird's-eye view of the harbour, take the lift to the observation deck of the 106m (348ft) **Marine Tower**. The beacon atop the tower gives it a claim of being the tallest lighthouse in the world; it also has an interesting oceanographic museum.

The Minato Mirai 21 project, launched in the mid-1980s, was intended to turn a huge tract of neglected waterfront north and east of Sakuragi-cho into a model 'city of the future', integrating business, exhibition and leisure facilities. The centrepiece of the project is the 70-storey **Landmark Tower**, Yokohama's tallest building; its observation deck (daily 10am–9pm, Sat until 10pm; www.yokohama-landmark.jp) affords a spectacular view of the city and the Bay Bridge, especially at night.

The nearby **Yokohama Museum of Art** (Fri–Wed 10am–6pm; www.yaf.or.jp/yma), designed by Tange Kenzo, houses works by both Western and Japanese artists, including Picasso, Braque, Kandinsky, Kishida Ryusei and Yokoyama Taikan. On the waterfront itself is **Nippon-maru Memorial Park** and **NYK Maritime Museum** (Tue–Sun 10am–5pm), where pride of

At the entrance to Yokohama's Chinatown, the largest in Japan

place goes to the three-masted sailing ship, popularly called the 'Swan of the Pacific', which is open to visitors for guided tours. A short walk from here, across the Kisha-Michi Promenade, takes you to Shinkocho, a man-made island which features **Akarenga Park** and the **Red Brick Warehouse**, a row of old redbrick custom houses that now serve as shops, restaurants and boutiques.

Yokohama's Chinatown, a few minutes' walk from Japan Railways' Kannai Station in the centre of the city, is the largest in Japan. Its narrow alleys are crowded with shops selling foodstuffs, spices, herbal medicines, cookware – in fact, anything that China exports. The restaurants, needless to say, are wonderful.

Fashionable, upbeat Yokohama is centred in two areas. One is Basha-michi ('Horse-Carriage Street') running from Kannai Station

Big wheel

The Cosmo Clock 21 Ferris Wheel, at 112.5m (369ft) one of the largest in the world, offers fabulous views of the Minato Mirai complex. A full turn of the wheel takes 15 minutes.

to the waterfront. The street acquired its name in the 19th century, when it was laid out for the vehicles of the city's Western residents; a more recent redesign evokes that era with red-brick pavements and imitation gas lamps – but the boutiques along the street are up-to-the-minute. The other area extends from Ishikawa-cho Station to Motomachi and the International Cemetery. Motomachi was the first area developed in the Meiji period to serve Western shoppers, and it has kept pace with the movements of fashion ever since.

The **Foreigners' Cemetery**, established in 1854, is the last resting place of some 4,000 foreigners of 40 different nationalities who lived and died in Yokohama. Behind it is the Yamate Shiryokan, a small museum (Tue–Sun 10am–5pm) of materials about the city's 19th-century European population. Just up the hill at this end of Motomachi is Harbour View Park, where the views at night – when Yamashita Park and the harbour are floodlit – are especially fine.

Just beneath the cemetery, the elevated bluff known as the Yamate was considered a desirable place to live by foreigners and diplomats, who built colonial-style residences here. Several have survived. The **Yamate Museum**, close to an English church, provides a good overview of the history of the area.

The last must-see in Yokohama is **Sankeien** (daily 9am–5pm; www.sankeien.or.jp), originally the estate of wealthy silk merchant and art connoisseur Hara Sankei, who opened his garden to the public in 1906. At great expense he transferred here a number of important 17th-century buildings that once belonged to the Tokugawa family, including the Rinshunkaku villa and the charming Choshukaku tea pavilion, as well as a small temple from Kyoto's famed Daitokuji. Sankei-en is a special delight from February though early April, when the plum and cherry trees blossom.

Kamakura

Kamakura, less than an hour south of Tokyo by train, was the seat of Japan's first military government. The Kamakura shogunate was founded late in the 12th century after a long and bloody rivalry between two noble factions over control of the imperial court. The victorious Minamoto clan chose **Kamakura** as its headquarters because this fishing village – girded on three sides by steep wooded hills and on the fourth by the Pacific Ocean – was a natural fortress.

Here they created what most of us envision as the 'Way of the Samurai': the values, codes, religion and culture of a warrior caste that would rule Japan for 700 years. Much of that culture was inspired by the Rinzai sect of Zen Buddhism and its sense of discipline and self-control, its austere philosophy of art and life. The shogunate founded great numbers of Zen temples in Kamakura. Many are still standing, and some are registered as National Treasures. From the Japan Railways station at Kita (North) Kamakura, about an hour from Tokyo on the Yokosuka line, you can easily reach six of these temples.

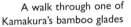

A walk through one of Kamakura's bamboo glades

Engakuji was founded in 1282 for the souls of those killed during the unsuccessful Mongol invasion the previous year. It became the second most important in the group of monasteries called the Gozan ('Five Mountains'), a hierarchy established in the 14th century for the Zen temples under the official patronage of the shogunate. Engakuji

Dancer at Hachimangu

is Kamakura's largest temple complex; often wracked by fire and earthquake, 17 of the original 46 buildings have survived. Two of these are registered as National Treasures: the *shariden* (hall of holy relics), built in 1282, and the huge belfry on the hill above. The bell, 2.5m (8ft) tall, was cast in 1301. The principal building open to the public at Engakuji is the *butsunichi-an* ceremonial hall, where visitors can take part in a tea ceremony.

Nearby is **Tokeiji**, familiarly known as the 'Divorce Temple', which was unique as a sanctuary for the women of the warrior caste seeking an escape from unhappy marriages. If the victim managed to make her way here and stay for three years as a nun, she could obtain a decree of divorce from the shogunate and go free. The *homotsukan* (treasure house) of Tokeiji has a collection of Kamakura-period paintings, sculpture and calligraphy, some of which are registered as Important Cultural Objects. Also in the grounds is the Matsugaoka Bunko, a research library established in memory of D.T. Suzuki (1870–1966), who pioneered the study of Zen Buddhism in the West.

South of Tokeiji, on the way to Kamakura's centre, are Meigetsu-in and Jochiji, Zen temples with especially fine gardens. Still further south is **Kenchoji**, founded in 1253, the foremost of the 'Five Mountains'. It was modelled on one of the great Chinese monasteries of the time and built for a Chinese monk who was said to have interceded with the dreaded Kublai Khan to stop the

Mongol invasion of Japan. Kenchoji is still an active monastery; like many of the temples in Kamakura, it offers visitors the opportunity to take part in Zen meditation training sessions. Nearby Ennoji boasts a remarkable group of sculptures representing Enma (the Lord of Hell) and his judges.

Sightseeing in Kamakura

If you arrive at Kamakura station, turn left and explore two fascinating streets. The larger, **Wakamiya-dori**, is lined with cherry trees, traditional restaurants and confectionary stores, as well as the town's trademark *kamakura-bori* lacquerware. Parallel **Komachi-dori** is a pedestrian street jammed with intriguing souvenir shops, restaurants and speciality shops selling incense, stones and papercraft.

Both streets lead to **Tsuru-ga-oka Hachimangu**, the shrine complex built by Yoritomo no Minamoto, the first Kamakura shogun. It was dedicated to the legendary Emperor Ojin, from whom Yoritomo claimed descent. As part of the mid-September festival

Shizuka's Dance

The Hachimangu shrine was the scene of many dramatic incidents, including the assassination of Sanetomo, Yoritomo's second son and the last Minamoto shogun, by his own nephew – the priest, Kugyo. A ginkgo tree by the shrine's main hall marks where the murder took place.

The most poignant tale, however, is associated with the so-called Maiden Hall. Once installed as shogun, Yoritomo fell out with his dashing half-brother Yoshitsune, whom he believed was plotting against him, and sent him into exile. Yoshitsune's lover, Shizuka, was brought to Hachimangu and commanded to dance at the shrine as penance. What she performed, however, was a dance of defiance and love for Yoshitsune. When Yoritomo discovered that Shizuka was carrying Yoshitsune's child, he ordered it killed at birth. But the outcome of this story is lost in legend. Some versions assert that the child was indeed slain; others say it was placed in a cradle, like Moses, and cast adrift in the reeds.

Photo opportunity in front of the stone bridge at Hachimangu

at this shrine, there is a spectacular tournament of archery on horseback *(yabusame)*, in which contestants dressed in the costume of Kamakura-period huntsmen must hit a series of three small wooden targets as they come down a narrow course at full gallop. The spacing between the targets gives the rider just barely enough time to drop the reins, notch and fire an arrow and regain control of his mount.

Close to the shrine are two museums. The **Kamakura Municipal Museum of Modern Art** (Tue–Sun 9.30am–5pm) houses a collection of Japanese oil paintings, watercolours, wood-block prints and sculpture. The **Kokuhokan** (National Treasure Museum; Tue–Sun 9am–4pm) has a fine collection of objects from various Kamakura temples and shrines, including some excellent 13th-century paintings.

A 10-minute walk east of the Hachimangu, across a shallow stream on the right is **Takedera**, better known as the 'Bamboo Temple'. Located in the midst of a small but dense bamboo grove, the temple has a delightful pavilion where visitors can enjoy a bowl of thick green *matcha*, the green brew served in the tea ceremony.

Opposite, along Kamakura-kaido, **Sugimoto-dera** is an ancient thatched temple whose dark interior oozes with the mysteries of esoteric Buddhism. **Jomyo-ji**, another fine temple, is just next door. In the back streets to the east, climb a wooded path to **Zuisen-ji**, where there are quiet, lush gardens at the front of the temple and a severe, dry landscaped area incorporating part of a cave at the rear.

Yoritomo was determined to create a 'Seated Buddha' for his capital to rival the huge bronze figure made in 749 for Todaiji temple in Nara. That idea bore fruit in 1252 with the casting of the 125-tonne **Daibutsu** in the courtyard of Kotoku-in temple – after Mt Fuji, probably the most photographed icon of Japan. The massive seated figure, 11.4m (37ft) high, sits in the classical pose of the Amida Buddha ('Compassionate One'), his hands resting in his lap, the thumbs touching the palms and the eyes half-closed in an expression of profound serenity. The statue is hollow, and you can climb a staircase inside to look out through a window between the Buddha's shoulders. A temple was originally built to house the figure, but this structure was destroyed in a tidal wave in 1495. For the five centuries since then, the Buddha has been dispensing his benevolence to visitors in the open air.

Offering fruit and flowers at the foot of Daibutsu

The Daibutsu and Kotoku-in temple are in Hase, the district in the western part of Kamakura. The other major attraction here is **Hasedera**. In the Kannon Hall of this temple is the largest wooden devotional figure in the country: a statue of the 'Eleven-Faced Goddess of Mercy', some 10m (33ft) high, carved from a single tree trunk and covered in gold leaf. The 10

smaller heads in her crown symbolise her ability to search in all directions for those in need of compassion. No one knows for certain when the figure was carved; one legend dates it to the early 8th century. The Amida Hall of Hasedera houses the image of a seated Amida Buddha, endowed by Minamoto no Yoritomo when he was 42 – a particularly unlucky age according to popular Japanese belief.

Ryukoji Temple and Enoshima Island

Kamakura history was not shaped by the Minamoto clan alone. No account of this area would be complete without the story of Nichiren (1222–82), the monk who founded the only native Japanese sect of Buddhism. Nichiren's defiance of both Zen and Jodo ('Pure Land') Buddhism eventually persuaded the shogunate to order him beheaded on a hill to the south of Hase. However, legend says that, just as the executioner raised his sword, a lightning bolt struck and broke it in two. Before he could try again, a messenger arrived with an order commuting Nichiren's sentence to exile on the island of Sadogashima. Later, in 1337, the Nichiren sect built the **Ryukoji** temple on the same hill.

> **Katase**
>
> Benton Bridge connects Enoshima to the resort of Katase. Kabuki actors and others from the entertainment world often pray before the Hadaka (Naked) Benten statue, as she is the patroness of beauty, music and the arts.

On the nearby Sagami bay shore are Yuigahama and Shichirigahama, two of the beaches closest to the metropolitan area. In the hot, humid summer months it can feel as if the entire population of Tokyo and Yokohama is here, searching in vain for a vacant patch of sand. Equally popular is **Enoshima**, the little island just offshore, with a hill in the middle that affords – on clear days – a fine view of Mt Fuji and the Izu Peninsula. From Enoshima you can take the quaint old **Enoden-line**, which is part train, part tram, back to Kamakura station.

Hakone

Hakone is a national park and resort area southeast of Mt Fuji, extremely popular with weekend trippers from Tokyo. Just 90 minutes by train from the city, this area makes a pleasant daytrip. But to enjoy more of the countryside, you can stay overnight and continue down the Izu Peninsula the next day.

Even if you have a Japan rail pass, we suggest that you invest in the all-inclusive 'Hakone Free Pass' offered by the Odakyu Railway. This entitles you to a roundtrip train ticket from Shinjuku to Gora, connecting with the funicular railway up into the mountains to a cable car. You then swing across the volcanic Owakudani Valley and down the other side for a boat cruise across Lake Ashi to Hakone-machi. From there, you can take a bus (still on the same pass) along the Sumiko River to Odawara, and then back by train to Tokyo.

Among the many attractions of this excursion is the **Hakone Open-Air Museum** (Chokoku no mori, or 'Forest of Sculptures'; daily 9am–5pm; www.hakone-oam.or.jp) at Miyanoshita. Established in 1969, the museum rejoices in a wonderfully designed and landscaped mountain setting. Here the works of such Western sculptors as Moore, Arp, Calder and Giacometti share the garden space with those of Shimizu Takashi, Takamura Kotaro and other Japanese artists. The exhibits are chosen for their resis-

Icarus, in Hakone's enticing 'Forest of Sculptures'

tance to the elements, and the museum is as lovely in winter as it is in summer. The Meiji era resort town of Miyanoshita is also known as the home of the **Fujiya Hotel**, Japan's oldest European-style accommodation. Stop here for morning coffee or afternoon tea in the wood-panelled Orchid Room which looks over the hotel's fine Japanese garden.

Visitors stop here on the way to the little town of Gora, to catch the cable car to Sozan and from there the gondola ride up into the mountains and across the smoking, sulfurous Owakudani Valley. Escape the sulphur-impregnated air when you arrive in Gora by visiting the **Pola Museum of Art** (daily 9am–5pm; www.pola museum.or.jp), located in a lovely glass building in the forest. Japanese paintings and ceramics are included along with a collection of European artists including Cezanne, Monet and Van Gogh.

Take the next cable car to the shore of **Lake Ashi**, where excursion cruisers leave from the piers at Togendai for the 20-minute ride to Hakone-machi on the other side of the lake. On

Cable car above Owakudani Valley

a good day the reflection of Mt Fuji in these clear blue waters is breathtaking. In early August the resorts on the lakeshore sponsor the dramatic Torii Matsuri festival, when a great wooden arch is set alight and a thousand burning lanterns are sent floating out across the water.

In the Tokugawa period Hakone-machi was an important town on the Tokaido, the only highway through this mountainous area between the imperial court in Kyoto and the shogunal capital in Edo. The shogunate, always suspicious of people on the move, maintained a system of garrisons along the road, and no one went through without an official pass. The checkpoint here, called the **Hakone Sekisho**, is an exact replica of the original, with a small museum of period costumes and weapons. The surrounding area is well known for its inns and thermal baths and for its Hakone-zaiku woodcrafts with inlaid mosaic and marquetry.

Izu Peninsula

The jumping-off point for this popular holiday area is the town of Atami, about an hour from Tokyo on the *shinkansen* superexpress train. The **Izu Peninsula** is blessed with a sunny climate, fine beaches, picturesque little fishing ports and – perhaps more to the point – some of the country's best hot springs resorts.

Stretching south of the peninsula are the **Izu Shichito** (Izu Seven Islands). This chain of volcanic islands, each with a different topography and character, is easily accessed by boat and plane. Besides tranquillity, people come here for deep-sea fishing, snorkelling among the clear waters, surfing and for the hot thermals and rock pools that provide opportunities for fresh and salt-water bathing.

Two of the resort towns are of special interest to Westerners. **Ito**, about 16km (10 miles) south of Atami on the east coast, is a spa with some 800 thermal springs and good surf swimming along its beautiful, rugged coast. The nearby Omura-san Park has 3,000 cherry trees, with varieties blooming at different times of year. Historically, Ito was home for five years to William Adams, the Englishman shipwrecked on the shores of Kyushu in the early 17th century who became an advisor to Tokugawa Ieyasu. For his knowledge of seafaring, he was given the title *anjin* ('pilot'). At Ieyasu's command, Adams (the model for the hero of James Clavell's novel *Shogun*) set up a shipyard in Ito and built Japan's first two European-style ocean-going vessels. There is a monument to Adams at the mouth of the Okawa River, and the Anjin Festival is held in his honour every August.

Shimoda, at the southern tip of the peninsula, is famous in still another historical context. It was off the coast here that Commodore Matthew Perry, ordered by the US government to open diplomatic relations with Japan by force if necessary, anchored his fleet of black ships. The shogunate bowed to the pressure and agreed to accept American diplomat Townsend Harris, who established the first US consulate at Gyokusenji temple in Shimoda in 1856. Two years later, at nearby Ryosenji temple, negotiations resulted in the first US–Japan Treaty of Amity and Commerce. The monument to Perry and Harris, not far from the harbour, celebrates these epoch-making events, as does Shimoda's annual Kurobune Matsuri ('Black Ship Festival') in May.

In fact, charming though it still is today as a fishing port and yacht harbour, Shimoda was worthless from the commercial or diplomatic perspective. The shogunate had simply stuck Harris there to keep the dreaded Westerners away from the capital. Later, he negotiated the opening of Yokohama as a trading port and foreign settlement. Such was the subsequent dismay among reactionary factions at this sign of weakness that the Tokugawa shogunate was soon overthrown.

Rowing on a lake below the snowcapped peak of Mt Fuji

Mt Fuji

Most of the world's national symbols – the Statue of Liberty, the Eiffel Tower, the Kremlin, the Great Wall – are man-made. Japan's is a phenomenon of nature. And yet, in its near perfect symmetry, the cone of **Mt Fuji**, snowcapped even in summer, is so exquisitely formed that it seems more like the work of an infinitely patient landscape artist than a volcanic accident. The solitary majestic peak rises 3,776m (12,385ft) into the heavens. It is, in a word, simply beautiful. Here, more than in any temple garden or ancient castle ground, you can appreciate why the Japanese prefer to blur the distinction between nature and art.

The volcano's name is thought to derive from an Ainu word for 'fire'. Fuji-san last erupted in 1707, and today only an occasional puff of steam breaks through its crust, the fitful snore of a sleeping giant. Graciously, it remains dormant for the sake of the hundreds of thousands of visitors who come every year to climb to the summit. For some, the climb is an act of piety: the mountain is revered as the abode of Japan's ancestral gods.

Mt Fuji in winter

For others, the climb is an exercise in self-discipline and physical purification. Still others come out of no particular religious impulse, on holiday, making the ascent mainly to be able to say they've done it and leaving – almost in spite of themselves – with a profound sense of spiritual uplift. No travel brochure can make Mt Fuji a cliché, nor can the most jaded of world travellers remain immune.

Most visitors begin their climb at Kawaguchi Lake, in the resort area north of the mountain, getting that far by train from Tokyo in about two hours. The official climbing season is 1 July to 27 August, although mountain huts at each of the 10 stations on the various routes of ascent are open from April to mid-November. Climbing 'out of season' (especially in wet weather) is not recommended, but people do it all the time.

From Kawaguchi, you take a local bus to Go-gome ('Fifth Station') on the north face, to start the five-hour hike to the summit. There's also a direct bus to this point from the Shinjuku bus terminal in Tokyo that takes about two and a half hours. If you're coming from Kyoto or Osaka, the train or bus connections bring you to the Fujino-miya trail on the south face.

Truly dedicated pilgrims begin the climb around midnight, reaching the top in time to greet the sunrise. There's no danger of losing the well-marked trail, and the night ascent obviates the need to put up at any of the dormitory-style mountain huts along the way (where the accommodation is truly awful). You can stop at the seventh or eighth station to rest en route. Pack extra-warm clothing and wear good hiking boots, hats and gloves. Bad junk food from vending machines is all that's available at the summit, so it's best to bring your own supplies and, above all, a thermos of hot tea or coffee.

Fuji-san is like any other mountain in one respect: it's a lot easier coming down. More adventurous visitors will take the descent down the volcanic sand slide called the *suna-bashiri* to Shin-Gogome ('New Fifth Station'). Just sit on your backpack or a piece of cardboard, push off and slither down. From Shin-Go-gome, buses connect to the town of Gotemba for connections home.

Don't confine your visit to the mountain only. The **Fuji Five Lakes** that form a crescent around the north side of the peak offer delightful opportunities for fishing, boating and hiking. Yamanaka-ko is the largest of the five. Kawaguchi-ko is the most popular, probably because of the excursion boats that ply the route along the north shore, where – with luck and good weather – you get a perfect mirror-image reflection of Mt Fuji in the water. Sai-ko has the best trout fishing, and Shoji-ko is smallest, prettiest and still relatively undeveloped. Motosu-ko is the clearest and deepest of the five.

Between Sai-ko and Shoji-ko lies the dense, mysterious **Jukai** ('Sea of Trees'), a forest notorious for being easier to enter than to leave. The volcanic substrata here throw magnetic compasses completely out of whack. Many holiday visitors lose their way, some of them on purpose: the eerie Jukai is a perennial favourite with would-be suicides, and every year the local authorities conduct a sweep of the forest to recover the bodies that would otherwise never be discovered. Due south of Motosu-ko, the glistening white 26m (85ft) Shiraito Falls make a far more cheerful setting for a picnic.

KANSAI

Embracing the historical and cultural centres of Kyoto and Nara, the Ise-Shima shrines, and the vibrant commercial cities of Osaka and Kobe, the **Kansai** region is essentially the heart of the nation.

Shrine and temple

Shrines are always Shinto, while temples are Buddhist. The suffixes *-jinja, -jingu* and *-gu* indicate a shrine, whereas *-tera, -dera* and *-ji* are used to designate temples.

While Tokyo usually provides the first glimpse of modern Japan's many strange contrasts, it is to Kyoto and Nara that visitors with even a passing interest in Japanese history and culture come to peel back the layers of centuries. Although Kyoto is internationally renowned as the country's *de facto* cultural capital, nearby Nara was the first important home of the imperial court and still boasts many of Japan's most important temples and shrines.

Ise-Shima National Park is the supreme sanctuary of Japan's ancestral Shinto deities. Osaka and neighbouring Kobe offer striking perspectives of modern commercial Japan, albeit on a more accessible and less intimidating scale than Tokyo's sprawling urban conglomeration. No other region of Japan offers the same combination of urban intensity, rural tranquillity and dramatic cultural treasures – and all in such close proximity. Try to pick up a copy of the monthly English-language *Kansai Time Out* magazine for listings of events in the region.

Kyoto

 For millions of would-be travellers around the world, the very name **Kyoto** conjures up images of the exotic and the foreign. Here you will find magnificent temples, shrines and pagodas; exquisite Zen gardens; sumptuous traditional feasts; and, of course, that most alluring and misunderstood of creatures – the kimono-clad geisha. Kyoto is the national centre for such traditional disciplines as *chado* (tea ceremony) and *ikebana* (flower arranging), the birthplace of *kabuki and* the leading centre of calligraphy, painting and sculpture.

The city has a unique place in the Japanese national identity, and one-third of Japan's entire population is estimated to visit the city each year. Despite this, in many ways Kyoto is a surprisingly typical modern Japanese city, with the usual nondescript concrete buildings along with the remarkable pockets of culture and beauty.

For a thousand years, Kyoto served as the cultural and spiritual capital of Japanese civilisation, the home of its revered emperors after the Nara period from the end of the 8th century up to the Meiji Restoration in the late 19th century. The imperial rulers moved the capital to Kyoto originally to escape from the growing domination of the Buddhist authorities of Nara. In the new capital the building of Buddhist temples was actually briefly banned – ironic in a city now universally renowned for its temples.

Kyoto simply means 'Capital City', though it was originally known as Heian-kyo ('Capital of Peace'), the name given to the golden Heian era between the 10th and 12th centuries. During this time Kyoto thrived as Japan's cultural and creative heartland. But

Imperial Palace in the ancient capital, Kyoto

In Kyoto, geisha are called *geiko*, meaning 'art lady'

the city's fortunes turned during the Warring States period (1467–1568), which was finally brought to an end by the unifying warlords Nobunaga and Hideyoshi in the middle of the 16th century.

In many ways, the city has never recovered from Hideyoshi's subsequent decision to move the national capital from Kyoto to Edo (now Tokyo) in the early 1600s – a blow compounded by the young Emperor Meiji shifting the imperial household to Tokyo in 1868. But Kyoto has nevertheless remained the repository of the nation's noblest cultural pursuits and architectural legacy.

Kyoto's Imperial Residences

The Imperial Palace (Kyoto Gosho) and the Katsura and Shugakuin imperial villas are mandatory destinations for anyone with even a shred of interest in Japanese architecture, design and aesthetics. However, since they are imperial property, special reservations must be made with the Kyoto office of the Imperial Household Agency, which dictates every nuance and moment of the imperial family's life. The agency is located in the grounds of the Imperial Palace, just south of Imadegawa-dori; applicants must be 18 or over, passports are required. Reservations can also be made at http://sankan.kunaicho.go.jp.

Fires ravaged Kyoto's original 8th-century **Imperial Palace**, and the present buildings are a 19th-century reconstruction. Through the western Seishomon Gate is the Shishinden ceremonial hall, where emperors are enthroned – a privilege retained by Kyoto after the move to Tokyo – and where New Year's audiences are held. To the west is the cypress-wood Seiryoden (the 'Serene and Cool Chamber'), the emperor's private chapel, serene and cool indeed in vermilion, white and black.

If you must visit only one of the two imperial villas, **Katsura** is the ultimate 'must see' in a city full of them. Conceived with meticulous care, Katsura is one of Japan's masterpieces of subtle residential design and garden landscaping. Every wall in the villa's seven pavilions is a sliding panel that can be opened to survey the surrounding landscape, including the gardens themselves and the Arashiyama Hills beyond. The Furushoin pavilion's verandah is the perfect place for viewing the full moon.

Those Enigmatic Geisha

Few aspects of Japanese life are more elusive than the geisha. You may see cheap imitations in expensive nightclubs on Tokyo's Ginza or even a real one being driven past in a limousine on the way to an exclusive party. But as a non-Japanese, you are unlikely to see an authentic geisha first-hand unless you find yourself the guest of a Japanese businessman with a fat expense account. It is usually unheard of for them to perform for unescorted foreigners, who are not considered sufficiently versed in Japanese ways to appreciate this institution.

The word geisha means 'art person' – in Kyoto, as befits the old imperial capital, she's more elegantly known as *geiko* ('art lady'). She has the sophisticated talents of a singer, dancer, actress and musician. A girl is taken on in her teens as an apprentice and is trained by older geisha in the traditional arts of entertaining Japanese men who want to spend an evening in a teahouse, away from their wives.

Contrary to popular conception, a geisha is not a glorified prostitute. A genuine geisha has the prestige and admiration accorded to actresses or singers at the top of their profession in the West. Charm and personality are considered more important than physical beauty. A true geisha is primarily a highly trained professional entertainer, hired on the basis of her charm and skills.

The **Shugakuin** imperial villa lies at the foot of sacred Mt Hiei. Its spacious grounds are a magnificent example of the 'strolling' gardens favoured during the Edo period. Built by the shogun in the 17th century for an abdicated emperor, Shugakuin is in fact three villas, each with airy teahouses in the gardens. The upper villa – grandest of the three – dominates an imposing avenue of pines.

Exploring the City

Kyoto is a surprisingly large metropolis. Since its numerous attractions are spread evenly throughout the city, good maps are essential. The city has two subway lines, several small private railway lines and many bus routes. If you don't want to depend on costly taxis, make sure you have a bus map, which can be picked up at the tourist information offices in Kyoto Station or at any JNTO office. However, with over 1,500 Buddhist temples, 200 Shinto shrines, numerous museums and magnificent imperial palaces, be aware that you're not going to see everything.

Try to get hold of the *Kyoto Visitor's Guide,* a free glossy monthly packed with listings of cultural events and information on temples, gardens, festivals, exhibitions, restaurants and even accommodation. Sampling Kyoto is definitely a case of 'less is more', and the secret is to pace yourself.

Higashiyama

On the city's east side, **Higashiyama** has temples, theatres, museums and parks – a fine introduction to exploring the imperial city on foot.

Kiyomizu temple, one of Kyoto's oldest, is so popular that on Sundays it offers all the serenity of rush hour at Kyoto's garish station. But don't let that put you off. Founded in 788 just before the city entered its golden age as the imperial capital, its numerous buildings nestle lovingly against steep Mt Higashiyama in a dramatic cascade of thatched and tiled roofs. However, most of what we see today is actually a 17th-century reconstruction of the original 8th-century structure. With its numerous buildings set within extensive grounds, Kiyomizu's main attraction is the *hondo* (main hall). This elevated structure's projecting wooden terrace is supported by a vast arrangement of 139 massive interlocking beams. Across on the mountainside is another terrace on which imperial courtiers and dignitaries would sit while enjoying dance performances and music recitals on the *hondo's* broad terrace. (The popular expression 'to jump from Kiyomizu's terrace' means to do something daring and adventurous.)

Steps lead down from Kiyomizu's main hall to Otowa-no-taki, a waterfall where visitors sip water from a spring said to have many health benefits, if not sheer divine power for the true believer. A short walk leads up the other side of the valley to a small pagoda with a view encompassing the entire hillside.

Crowds flock to Kiyomizu to take in the bright yet delicate hues of cherry blossoms in spring or the blaze of red and gold maple

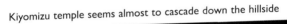

Kiyomizu temple seems almost to cascade down the hillside

leaves in autumn, with special night-time illuminations (check at any tourist office for dates and times).

A moderate stroll takes you to Higashiyama's **Gion** district, Kyoto's main historical centre of traditional theatre, arts and (now) antiques. It is especially renowned as the last centre of training for the city's most celebrated residents, the geisha. This is the place to wander and soak up the sights and sounds of Kyoto's lone quarter still dedicated to traditional arts and entertainment. Your curiosity and patience may reward you with a glimpse of a genuine geisha or *maiko* (apprentice geisha), the copious layers of her opulent – and unimaginably heavy – silk kimono rustling as she hurries to an appointment or a training session.

Gion is a global magnet for collectors and dealers of Japanese antiques. Prices are usually high. But even if you're not in

Kyoto Festivals

The Japanese, especially in Kyoto, define their year with festivals and rituals. The following is a selection:

April: Local *geisha* in opulent costumes perform traditional dances at the Gion Kobu Kaburenjo theatre in Gion. Kyoto has a multitude of lively blossom-viewing *(hanami)* parties, the most famous being Daigoji.

June: Kifune-jinja, dedicated to the god of water, celebrates the season in a vibrant water festival. Torchlight performances of *Noh* plays.

July: The biggest festival in Kyoto is the Gion Matsuri, dating from the 10th century. On 17 July decorative floats parade through town.

October: A month of festivities. The Bull Festival at Koryuji is known as one of the 'Weird Festivals' of Kyoto. Jidai Matsuri (Festival of the Ages) climaxes the Weird Festivals and apexes October's round of fancy dress. Some 2,000 participants lead a parade through town representing famous people in Japanese history.

December: Face-showing *(kaomise)* is Kyoto's gala *kabuki* performance at Minami-za, when the actors reveal their real faces. Senbon Shaka-do celebrates Buddha's enlightenment with a radish-boiling ceremony!

the market for a major investment, browsing for antiques is a marvellous way to get a real taste of Japan's celebrated traditional design and aesthetics. Some shops are more like small museums, offering exquisite examples of the finest craftsmanship.

A *maiko* walks through the narrow streets of Gion

The 17th-century Minamiza Theatre – Japan's oldest – stages the famous Kaomise *kabuki* show in December. But foreign visitors can enjoy the **Gion Corner**, held at Yasaka Hall to provide a selection of bite-sized samples of Japanese culture from March to November. In a comfortable little theatre you can watch a one-hour demonstration of the tea ceremony, traditional music and dance, flower arranging, puppet theatre and a *kyogen* farce. (Tickets for Gion Corner are usually available through your hotel or the Tourist Information Centre.)

At the northeast corner of Gion is **Maruyama Park**, one of Kyoto's most popular recreation areas and known for its beautiful garden and magnificent cherry blossoms in early April. It borders two important temples. The massive **Chioninji** is home to the Jodo ('Pure Land') Buddhist sect, which in the 12th century spread the appeal of Buddhism to the uneducated classes. Looming to an imposing height of 24m (79ft), its entrance gate is thought to be the largest structure of its kind in the world. The ringing of Chioninji's bell, Japan's largest and best known, is televised nationally when resident monks usher in the new year.

A huge arch *(torii)* spanning the main road marks the approach to the **Heian Shrine**. This popular shrine features a strongly Chinese-influenced design and an extensive landscaped garden considered one of Kyoto's finest, with numerous cherry trees and a large pond with an elegant pagoda linked to the shore by a covered bridge. In the vicinity are two absorbing museums reflecting Kyoto's extensive history as a magnet for Japan's finest craftsmen. The **Museum of Traditional Crafts** (daily 9am–5pm) presents a diverse collection of textiles, por-

All the World's a Garden

In a Japanese garden, every artifice is used to make things look 'natural'. By cunning use of proportion, designers are able to make a small space appear vast. Gardens may be formal, semiformal, or informal – the same concepts that characterise Japanese painting and flower arrangement.

Influenced by the Chinese, the Japanese have been designing gardens since the 6th century. Later, under the influence of the austere precepts of Zen Buddhism, gardens encouraged meditation, as in the peaceful rock-and-water garden of Kamakura's Zuisenji temple. The Zen garden reached its zenith in Kyoto with 'flat gardens' devoid of hills, bridges, or ponds – only rocks in white sand or gravel. The most famous is at Ryoan-ji temple, but equally admirable examples can be seen at Nanzenji's 'Leaping Tiger Garden' or Zuiho-in's 'Blissful Mountain'.

More elaborate designs evolved to incorporate existing natural features. The opulent Momoyama architecture at the end of the 16th century brought dramatic and colourful gardens with bizarrely shaped rocks and trees, as at Kyoto's Nishi-Honganji temple.

Edo (Tokyo) garden design became more utilitarian – with fruit trees to provide food and reeds for making arrows. Larger, so-called strolling gardens came close to the spirit of English parks, but still with deliberate aesthetic touches, as in the celebrated Kenrokuen Park *(see page 143)* in Kanazawa or the Ritsurin Park in Takamatsu on Shikoku Island.

Japanese gardens have something even for our industrial age. Offices sometimes have tray-gardens with miniature bonsai trees, pebble-rocks and even a tiny goldfish pond.

celain, fans, dolls, lacquerware, cutlery and cabinetwork, with occasional live demonstrations by craftsmen. Next door is the **National Museum of Modern Art** (Tue–Sun 9.30am–5pm; www.momak. go.jp). which is, despite its name, mainly devoted to 19th- and 20th-century ceramics.

Before exploring the Silver Temple, consider some of the quieter temple gardens in the northern section of the eastern foothills. A short walk from Shugakuin-michi bus stop (No. 5 City Bus), or the Eizan railway station of the same name,

Philosopher's Path, resplendent with cherry blossom in spring

takes you to **Manshuin**, a delightfully tranquil Tendai sect temple that dates from 1656. Maple and cherry trees stand on the fringe of an immaculately raked garden of sand and gravel. The walk south from here through a pleasant residential area takes you to the narrow, bamboo entrance to **Shisendo**, a rustic hermitage with an adjacent karensansui (dry landscape garden) bordered by azaleas, maples and persimmon. Another, often overlooked temple, **Kompukuji**, is a short walk from here. Another dry landscape garden with a steep bank of azaleas, this temple is affiliated with the Rinzai school of Zen, but also has literary associations with two of Japan's greatest haiku masters, Basho and Buson.

At the northern edge of Higashiyama is one of Japan's most famous and delightful short walks: the **Philosopher's Path** – named after the Japanese philosopher Nishida Kitaro – snakes about 2km (1¼ miles) along the bank of a narrow canal running between two major temples, Nanzenji and Ginkakuji. Despite the

Temple details at Nanzenji

large numbers who come to view the spring blossoms and the superb autumn leaves, the Philosopher's Path is one of Kyoto's most tranquil and beloved strolls. Any of the several friendly little teahouses and coffee shops along the way make an ideal rest stop.

Nanzenji is a former 13th-century palace whose precincts now house a dozen affiliated temples and monasteries. The great gate at the main entrance was built in 1628 and became notorious as the site where a robber named Goemon Ishikawa was boiled alive in an iron cauldron while holding his son aloft to save him from the same fate. Since then, old-fashioned Japanese iron bathtubs have been gruesomely known as 'goemon-buro'. The view from atop the 30m (98ft) gate provides a fine overall view of the temple grounds and sacred Mt Hiei to the north. The temple's truly unique feature is the large red-brick aqueduct behind the main buildings, which still carries water from Lake Biwa and is a popular strolling route for local residents.

A few minutes west of Nanzenji, the quiet **Murin-an** is a classic private villa with a stunning landscaped garden. The view towards the northeastern hills is sublime.

Also not far from Nanzenji is the wonderful **Eikan-do**, an exquisite temple set against the hillside. Its beautiful Amida Buddha statue is, unusually, turning to look back over its shoulder. Its strange posture commemorates a legendary statue that came to life and then berated Eikan, the astonished monk looking on, for pausing from his ritual chanting. Each autumn the temple has a special night-time illumination of its many maple trees, their flaming reds and oranges highlighted with strategically placed pin-spotlights. The effect is sublime and utterly unforgettable.

At the other end of the canal is the second major temple on the path. **Ginkakuji** (mid-Mar–Nov 8.30am–5pm, Dec–mid-Mar 9am–4.30pm), the famous 'Silver Pavilion,' never received the silver-leaf covering originally intended. It was built in the 15th century by an aesthete-mystic shogun, Yoshimasa Ashikaga, who used it for esoteric tea ceremonies and, above all, moon-watching in the elegant garden. Its flat-topped hillock of white gravel, despite the inevitable comparison to Mt Fuji, reputedly originated as a pile of sand left behind by the temple's construction workers.

It is a short bus ride to the **Kyoto National Museum** (Tue–Sun 9.30am–5pm), which houses the country's largest collection of Japanese sculpture and painting as well as weapons, traditional armour and 10 centuries of costume including some dazzling *noh* theatre costumes with masks. Most of this peerless collection has been gathered from the temples and palaces of Kyoto, Nara and other important cultural centres.

Just south of the National Museum is the spectacular **Sanjusangendo**, the 'Hall of Thirty-Three Bays'. The original temple built in 1164 survived only 100 years, and today's reconstruction dates from the 13th century. Its centrepiece is a gilded seated wooden statue of the Kannon Bodhisattva, 3.3m (11ft) high, with 11 faces on the crown of its head and 40 arms (extravagantly known as 'a thousand arms') wielding bells, wheels and lotus flowers. However, Sanjusangendo's main wonder is its legion of 1,000 gilded Kannon images flanking the central Buddha. The identical statues were carved by the 13th-century masters Kokei, Unkei and Tankei, with 70 assistants.

A slew of arrows

Archery has played a role at Sanjusangendo from the 17th century, when an archer is recorded as having fired 13,000 arrows in 24 hours; however, only 8,000 reached the target.

The enigmatic Zen garden at Ryoanji

Ukyo and Kita

Nestling in the northwest corner of Kyoto, **Ryoanji** (Mar–Nov 8am–5pm, Dec–Feb 8.30am–4.30pm; www.ryoanji.jp) is the best known of all Zen Buddhist temples. Its famous rock garden has provoked more debates – both admiring and critical – than there are chips of gravel in its rectangular 30m by 10m (98ft by 32ft) expanse. There are no trees and no shrubs, just 15 stark rocks embellished with ancient moss, standing in clusters amid the perfectly raked white gravel. Although it is usually attributed to the great master Soami, nobody knows for sure who created it – or why. The mystery surrounding its origins does nothing to undermine the power of its simplicity. Confounding interpretation, it epitomises the essence of Zen Buddhism's essentially anti-intellectual precepts. Dark islands in a white sea, or mountain peaks soaring above clouds: people see what they want to see. Get there early in the morning before the crowds arrive. Kyoto offers few more memorable experiences than secluded contemplation of Ryoanji's enigmatic rock garden.

Beyond the rock garden you can go for a walk among the maples and pines of the forest surrounding the lovely Kyoyochi Pond at the foot of Mt Kinugasa. Thick, luxuriant moss thrives throughout. Little known to foreign visitors, though just 15 minutes walk south, is the magnificent **Myoshinji**, a walled complex of temples, Japanese gardens and teahouses where you could easily spend a whole day.

From Ryoanji, a 20-minute stroll or a short bus ride takes you to **Kinkakuji** (daily 9am–5pm), Japan's famous 'Temple of the Golden Pavilion'. The original late 14th-century pavilion, completely covered in gold leaf, was typical of the unrestrained opulence of the Muromachi period favoured by Shogun Yoshimitsu Ashikaga, who had it built for his retirement at the ripe old age of 38. It was burned down by a fanatical young monk in 1950, rebuilt in 1955 as an exact replica of the original structure, and last renovated in 2002. Most of its buildings are closed to the public, but you pass an attractive thatch-roofed tea-ceremony house as you follow the winding stone steps towards the exit.

Another celebrated victim of fire is **Daitokuji**. This vast complex of 22 subtemples and affiliated monasteries (down from about 60 during the Edo period) was built, burned down and rebuilt between the 14th and 17th centuries. It is richly endowed with artistic treasures and some of Japan's most superb Zen gardens, reflecting its history as a renowned centre of calligraphy, gardening, tea ceremony and other refined arts. Four of Daitokuji's Zen subtemples in particular offer superb gardens, teahouses and artefacts. Daisen-in, the 'Zen Temple Without Equal', contains splendid painted *fusuma* (sliding panels) and wall paintings. Zuiho-in is a monastery whose curious gardens combine Zen Buddhist and Christian symbolism, together with both an attractive rock garden and an unusually geometric tea garden. Ryugen-in has five distinct rock gardens, one of which is apparently the smallest in Japan.

Samurai on screen

If you want a break from temples, try Toei Eigamur film studio. It specialises in the production of television films on the *samurai* and is open to the public.

Directly south of the complex lies the traditional weaving district of **Nishijin**. High quality textiles, including exquisite silk brocades, have been made here for centuries. The best place to hone up on the subject is the **Nishijin Textile Centre** (daily 9am–5pm).

To the west is **Kitano Tenmangu**, (daily 9am–5pm; www.kitano tenmangu.or.jp) a large and important shrine. Tenmangu shrines typically feature statues of seated cows and bulls believed to have healing properties. You will see people rubbing the part of a statue corresponding to an afflicted area in the hope of relief from pain and worry. The shrine is also known for its thousands of plum trees, whose deep pink blooms draw the crowds in the weeks preceding the annual cherry blossom frenzy. But the real crowds descend on the 25th of each month, when Kitano Tenmangu hosts its nationally famous flea market. People travel from afar to sift through used kimono, antique furniture and ceramics, antique scrolls, crafts, food and household items, paying prices ranging from the reasonable to the outrageous.

Nishi-Honganji is an excellent example of Japanese architecture

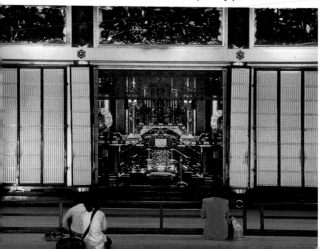

Central Kyoto

To the southwest of Kyoto Station is **Toji**, one of Kyoto's oldest temples, whose massive pagoda is the largest in Japan. Toji was established just after the imperial capital moved to Kyoto in 794, built with wood from sacred Mt Inari in the south. Thirty years later Kukai, the revered founder of esoteric Shingon Buddhism, was appointed head abbot. The temple complex quickly became Kyoto's main centre of Shingon Buddhism, which it remains today. In addition to its impressive pagoda, Toji is a national magnet for bargain hunters at its huge monthly flea market held on the 21st of each month.

> ## University town
>
> With some 40 universities, Kyoto is still considered Japan's centre of education. However, the number of students has recently gone down because of the lack of campus space. The exorbitant costs of building in the middle of the city has forced a number of faculties to decamp to the nearby countryside.

Just north of the tower are the headquarters of two schools of the Jodo-Shinshu ('Pure Land') sect, the Nishi-Honganji and Higashi-Honganji temples. The latter was built by Shogun Tokugawa Ieyasu to split and counteract the powerful influence of Nishi-Honganji, which had attracted thousands of followers with its free-wheeling Buddhism: it allowed priests to marry and have children, permitted the eating of meat and renounced traditional ascetic practices.

Most of **Higashi-Honganji** is closed to the public, but the main hall and founder's hall, rebuilt in 1895 after repeated fires, are notable for the rather unpleasant ropes of human hair fashioned from donations by female worshippers to haul the temple's pillars into position. Entrance to the temple's garden, the **Kikoku-tei** (9am–4pm), a short stroll east, is free. Shady and watered, this Japanese garden is a pleasant escape from the busy downtown area. There is much more to see in nearby **Nishi-Honganji**, a truly outstanding example of Japanese Buddhist monumental architecture, combining a bold, dramatic silhouette with rich ornamentation. The 17th-century buildings owe much of their splendour to the struc-

Emperor Meiji abolished the shogunate at Nijo Castle

tures brought here from Hideyoshi's opulent Fushimi Castle on the south side of Kyoto (dismantled by a Tokugawa shogun in 1632).

Nijo Castle is a poignant monument to the ironic twists of history. Built by Tokugawa Ieyasu in 1603 for his occasional, reluctant visits to Kyoto (under imperial command), the castle was taken over by the Emperor Meiji after the restoration of 1868. It was here that the emperor signed the edict abolishing the shogunate and sent his carpenters round the castle to replace the Tokugawa hollyhock crest with the imperial chrysanthemum.

Just east of the castle, the new **Kyoto International Manga Museum** (Tue–Thur 10am–8pm; www.kyotomm.com) proves that Kyoto is not just about the past. Billed as the world's only museum devoted exclusively to Japanese cartoons, visitors are allowed to take manga out onto the lawn and read them.

For a change of pace and mood, seek out **Nishiki Market**. This remarkably tranquil street market is housed under a single arcade. Note the colourful stands of dried fish and fresh fish, colourful pickles, stout young bamboo shoots, chicken wings and breasts arranged in elaborate patterns, and a whole cornucopia of squid, mussels, oysters and giant scallops.

Nearby, leading north from Shiji-dori, is another important market area worth exploring: **Teramachi** (literally, 'temple district'). Hideyoshi moved many of Kyoto's temples to this long narrow road during his reorganisation of the city in 1591 following its near-total destruction by clan warfare. Although small temples and shrines remain, visitors will enjoy exploring the covered shopping arcade between Shijo and Sanjo streets, famous for its second-hand bookshops, traditional hand-made paper *(washi)* shops, trendy but sometimes creative clothing stores and numerous pickle shops.

To the north of Oike, Teramachi becomes home to some of Kyoto's most respected antique and *washi* shops, some of which have been in business for hundreds of years. The adjoining streets comprise one of Japan's finest centres for buying traditional Japanese-style tables, screens, lamps, scrolls and other refined furnishings.

South Kyoto

It is impossible to overstate the importance of rice in Japanese culture. Each year in an important ceremony, the emperor plants rice in a symbolic field, reinforcing his role as the hereditary link between the Japanese people and their Shinto gods. So important is rice that it has the Shinto deity Inari all to itself. There are thousands of Inari shrines throughout Japan, distinguished by a pair of foxes standing guard.

Kyoto, however, boasts the most famous of them all – the **Fushimi-Inari Shrine** in southern Kyoto. In a city overpopulated by must-see attractions, this is one place guaranteed to deplete whatever superlatives re-

At the Fushimi-Inari Shrine

main in your exhausted vocabulary. The main shrine buildings are among Kyoto's most extensive, with rice and fox motifs everywhere. But take the path at the top right of the compound and you come to the first of Fushimi-Inari's remarkable features: its long, meandering tunnels of bright orange *torii* arches. Purchased by both companies and individuals (at vast expense) in the hope of incurring the blessings of the gods, the *torii* become smaller as you progress through the tunnel and begin to ascend the mountain. Further on you come to an amazing double tunnel, forcing you to choose the left or right paths. Along the way to the top of Mt Inari, you will pass many subshrines and countless bright red *torii* both minute and massive. Make sure you have plenty of film – you'll need it all.

One of the four extraordinary
Zen gardens at Tofukuji

North of Fushimi is **Tofukuji**, a
major Zen temple complex. In addition
to many impressive buildings, Tofukuji
offers four remarkable and distinctive
Zen gardens located in the *hojo* (abbot's
quarters). At Tofukuji's centre is a ravine
containing a small forest of maple trees.
Hundreds of thousands come each autumn to view the trees' spectacular
colours from the temple's covered
Tsutenkyo ('Heavenly Way Bridge').

Excursions from Kyoto

Arashiyama. When mind and body are
ready for a break from the rigours of
cultural sightseeing, head down to the
southern resort district of Arashiyama,
perched along the Hozu River (or the
Oi, as it's also known). The maple trees
setting off the river and the famous old
wooden Togetsukyo Bridge make it very popular with local tourists,
so it is worth avoiding on Sundays and public holidays.

Arashiyama is home to a number of important shrines and temples. The **Nonomiya Shrine** is uniquely renowned for its special
role in preparing imperial princesses to serve as vestal virgins at the
Grand Shrine of Ise, Japan's most important Shinto shrine *(see page
133)*. The shrine has a prominent role in the *Tale of Genji* and in
a famous *noh* play (entitled simply *Nonomiya*), and thus attracts
people with especial interest in classical Japanese literature.

Ohara. Also north of Kyoto is the rural enclave of Ohara, home
to the magnificent temple complex of **Sanzen-in**. From the bus
station, follow the signs in English pointing the way to the path

The mossy garden, part of the temple complex of Sanzen-in

that winds along a stream, past many stalls and small shops selling Ohara's famous pickles, to the temple's massive front gate.

The superbly landscaped Shuhekein pond garden is a legendary spot for meditation and contemplation. After the garden, venture into the hall at the end of the corridor and try your hand with a calligraphy brush along with the Japanese visitors writing traditional prayers to the central Amida Buddha. The view of the lush mossy landscaped garden from the verandah at the back of the building is one of Kyoto's most famous. The Ojo Gokurakuin hall at the temple's centre contains a magnificent seated Amida Buddha dating from 986 (and so revered that no photography is permitted). The stamps at the various numbered stations throughout the complex are particularly elegant and make a fine and unusual souvenir of your visit.

Miho Museum. Located some 30km (18½ miles) outside Kyoto, set deep in a forested nature preserve, is the Miho Museum (mid-Mar–mid-June, mid-July–mid-Aug and Sept–mid-Dec Tue–Sun 10am–5pm; www.miho.or.jp), designed by internationally acclaimed architect I.M. Pei. A tunnel leads to this outstanding privately owned collection of ancient Egyptian, South Asian, Chinese, Persian and, of course, Japanese masterworks. The building's exterior, interior and exhibit displays are triumphs of design and harmony between old and new, East and West, simplicity and complexity. The Miho should not be missed by anyone interested in Asian art and design.

Uji. Located on the JR Nara line, 30–40 minutes from Kyoto. Green hills stand as a backdrop to the majestic Uji River and the immensely important **Byodo-in**, a Unesco World Heritage site. Byodo-in's Phoenix Hall, with its gilded statue of Amida Buddha floating on a bed of lotuses, was built in the 11th century and has, against all the odds, survived intact. The first thing you will notice in Uji is the smell of roasting tea. Fragrant *uji-cha* was first planted in the 13th century. Uji green tea is now regarded as the finest in Japan.

Fukui

Just north of Kyoto is **Fukui**, a prefecture long renowned for its unique combination of history and superb natural scenery. For centuries it has been called the Echizen region, and that culturally significant name has definitely stuck. The Echizen coast includes famous columnar rock formations at Tojimbo and Sotomo, as well as some of Japan's finest beaches. Culinary delights include Echizen crab and distinctive Echizen *soba* (brown buckwheat noodles). And the simple, natural style of Echizen pottery has been popular throughout the country for hundreds of years, as have Echizen's highly regarded lacquerware and hand-crafted knives.

At **Ichidani** is a 16th-century village that served as the headquarters of the Asakura clan, which ruled Echizen until 1573. The painstakingly recreated buildings contain exhibits of the trades and crafts of the day, including a merchant's office and samurai homes.

In Fukui's far north, **Awara Onsen** has become one of Japan's most popular hot-spring resort towns since the emperor made it a hot spot for an imperial soak. But don't expect the rustic quaintness of traditional-style inns. Awara typically packs its heat-seekers into modern, luxury hotels whose harsh concrete exteriors hardly reflect the tranquillising pleasures provided within.

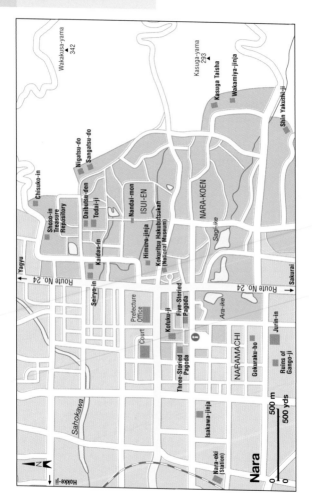

Nara

Nara

Although Kyoto remains the country's major cultural and historic destination, Japanese tourists equally revere Nara, the Kansai region's other celebrated historical centre. **Nara** was Japan's first imperial capital, and it remains home to many of its most important temples, shrines and collections of Buddhist art treasures. For anyone interested in Japanese history, art and culture, no visit to Japan could possibly be complete without a glimpse of Nara, however frustratingly brief. And, in addition to its magnificent cultural treasures, Nara offers the unlikely phenomenon of the world's most aggressive deer.

The Kintetsu Station is the ideal starting point for any exploration of the city. Next to the station's south entrance is an excellent tourist information centre. The friendly staff usually speak reasonable English and will happily ply you with maps and brochures, help you get oriented, and provide advice and information on festivals and special events. Next to the fountain outside Kintetsu Station is bustling Higashi-muki-dori, a covered mall of souvenir shops, antiques shops and numerous eateries. At the other end Sanjo-dori, Nara's main shopping street, has calligraphy stores noted for their fine inkstones, a Nara speciality.

Nara Park and Mt Wakakusa

The historic area of Nara is on the east side of the modern town, at the end of Sanjo-dori. **Naramachi** is a famous quarter filled with gorgeous historic houses, small shops, eclectic galleries and interesting museums. Here too is the western entrance to **Nara Park**, marking the boundary between urban sprawl and primal forest. The town's temples and shrines and a major museum are all in the park.

Nara Park's most famous residents are its deer, protected since the 8th century, when they were considered messengers from the gods. Despite being wild, the deer are quite tame and loiter around the park's various tourist attractions, hoping for a free snack of the deer biscuits sold here. Have your camera ready to record the incredible sight of a wailing Japanese child beating a hasty retreat to its parents after being chased by a group of hungry deer in a feeding frenzy.

Great clock at Nara Park's Todaiji temple complex

At the edge of Sarusawa-ike pond is **Kofukuji** temple. Its imposing 50m (166ft) five-storey pagoda, Japan's second-largest after Toji in Kyoto, is one of Nara's most photographed images. The present structure dates from 1426, replacing five earlier pagodas destroyed by fire. At its height Kofukuji embraced around 175 separate buildings, including the Kasuga Grand Shrine at the foot of Mt Wakakusa, with which it has been closely associated for 1,100 years. Kofukuji's many surviving artworks and artefacts are housed in its newest building, the Museum of National Treasures, a fire-proof repository built in 1958 to honour Kofukuji's immense cultural and historic importance.

Past Kofukuji is the original wing of the **Nara National Museum** (50 Noboriojicho; Tue–Sun 9am–5pm, Apr–Oct Fri until 7pm; www.narahaku.go.jp), linked by an underground passage to a newer, tile-roofed building just beyond it. This museum of ancient art focuses on Buddhist statues and sculptural styles from around 600 through the Middle Ages. The permanent collection is housed in the old wing, and its fascinating exhibits showcase the development of Chinese-influenced Buddhist art and design. The gift shop in the underpass between the two buildings offers an excellent selection of quality souvenirs, reproductions and posters of Nara culture.

Also on the west side of Nara Park is **Todaiji**, which – like many elaborate temple complexes – comprises many remarkable structures and artefacts. The first is the majestic Nandaimon (Great South Gate), standing over 19m (63ft) high and dating from 1199. Built in a classical Indian architectural style, this huge structure is only two-thirds the size of the original destroyed by a typhoon in 962. The gate houses the two Benevolent Kings, guardian deities created in the 12th century by master sculptors Unkei and Kaikei to guard the inner temple compound.

Pass through the gate for your first view of the massive roof of the Daibutsuden straight ahead. The current building, dating from 1709, is only two-thirds the size of the original, which burned down decades earlier, but even so it is now the world's largest wooden building. On the right of the door is Binzuru, a disciple of Prince Gautama (the Buddha's original name before achieving enlightenment). His statue is said to have special healing powers; sections of the statue shine with the polish of thousands – if not millions – of hands rubbing away ailments over the centuries. Finally, inside the massive hall, deep in meditation on a massive podium within a ring of giant lotus leaves, is Nara's celebrated **Daibutsu**, or Great Buddha. Nearly 15m (48½ft) tall, the gigantic cast-bronze statue is shorter than the original, unveiled in 752, when it was covered in gold leaf. As with all Buddha images, the positions of the hands are highly significant. The Great Buddha's

Todaiji's Daibutsu (Great Buddha) in meditative pose

Kasuga's Grand Shrine comes to life twice a year

right hand is bestowing spiritual tranquillity, while the left symbolises the granting of wishes. Seated on one side is the Nyorin Kannon, in whose hand is a jewel used to answer prayers and grant wishes; on the other is Kokuzo, who embodies wisdom and happiness.

To the east is **Nigatsu-do** (Second Month Hall), one of Todaiji's most famous subtemples, whose front portion rests on a vast network of wooden beams. The covered northern staircase and the broad stone southern staircase both lead up to the main walkway encircling the temple, which has massive lanterns and a strange assortment of artwork donated by supporting companies. Nigatsu-do hosts a spectacular fire purification festival in the second month of the lunar calendar (hence its name): the O-mizu Torii, or Water-Drawing Festival. Every night for two weeks, temple priests brandish long poles, each with a flaming cedar ball at the end. They run along the front of the verandah, deliberately showering the large crowd below with burning embers that are believed to bring good luck for the coming year, burning away transgressions from the previous one. Standing next door is Nara's oldest building, the **Sangatsu-do**, dating from AD729.

Along the foot of Mt Wakakusa is the **Kasuga Grand Shrine**, established to house the Shinto deities of the powerful Fujiwara family. It has been a place of worship for both emperors and aristocrats for centuries. The main approach from the east (from Kofukuji temple) is lined with thousands of stone lanterns set amid lush greenery. These are illuminated in dramatic crowd-drawing ceremonies held in early February and mid-August every year. The shrine's renowned Treasure House is one of the newest structures here, with wooden plaques in the shape of rice paddles reflecting the importance of rice in Shinto – and, by definition, Japanese – culture. A rice-planting ceremony is held in mid-March, during which the shrine's sacred rice field is symbolically replanted.

The **Kasuga Taisha Shin-en garden** (daily 9am–4pm), just before the entrance to the shrine, is a fascinating mix of formal garden, herbs, flowers and plants mentioned in the Nara- and Heian-period poetry anthology known as the *Manyoshu* ('Collection of Ten Thousand Leaves').

Directly south of the Kasuga Grand Shrine, the **Shin-Yakushi Temple** is an edifice of genuine antiquity. Founded by the Empress Komyo, the temple's hall, with an imposing collection of Buddhist statuary, is the original building, standing, in much the same manner as when it was erected in the 8th century, in a clearing of bush clover.

Outside Nara

South and west of modern Nara is an ancient area called Nishinokyo (meaning 'west of the capital'), where you will find three important temples. The sunset reflection of the twin pagodas of **Yakushiji** in a nearby lake is one of Japan's most striking and visually poetic im-

The Roots of Japanese Culture

Many consider Nara to be the root of Japanese culture and one of the cornerstones of Japan's unique forms of Buddhism. It began life in 710 as Heijo-kyo, meaning 'Citadel of Peace'. Originally a flat, nondescript tract of farmland in the Yamato Plain, it was selected as the site for a new imperial capital by the Emperor Mommu, just before his early death, and by Fujiwara-no-Fuhito, the head of the powerful aristocratic Fujiwara clan and father-in law of the succeeding emperor, Shomu. At the height of its glory, Heijo-kyo's skyline was punctuated by 50 pagodas, together with numerous temples, mansions and the imposing imperial court itself. Despite serving as Japan's imperial capital for only 74 years, Nara's influence on Japan's cultural development has loomed large throughout the city's 1,300-year history.

One of Yakushiji's twin pagodas, spectacularly illuminated

ages. Of the original buildings, only the To-to (East Pagoda) remains, considered by many to be Japan's most beautiful pagoda. Although it appears to have six storeys, the pagoda is actually a three-storey structure, each level having an extra roof for added visual impact. The vermilion Sai-to (West Pagoda) was built in 1980 on the site of the long-destroyed original. Between them is the Kondo (golden, or main, hall), reconstructed in 1975. Among its many notable bronze images is the Yakushi triad, comprising three blackened-bronze images: the Yakushi Buddha (dedicated to healing and medicine) seated on a medicine chest between Bodhisattvas of the sun and moon.

A 10-minute walk to the north is **Toshodaiji**, which boasts rare examples of ancient architecture and sculpture. Less spectacular than its expensively restored neighbour to the south, Toshodaiji nevertheless is the largest remaining example of Nara period architecture. Of its numerous period sculptures, the most celebrated is a 5m (16½ft) thousand-armed Kannon statue.

Every culture has a single historical hero, a visionary credited with planting the seeds from which cultural, aesthetic and ethical values flourished. For Japan, that person is the revered Prince Shotoku, early champion of Buddhism. Not only did this highly progressive leader produce Japan's first written constitution and legal code, thus laying the foundations of an organised state, he is also credited with having introduced the concept of *wa* ('harmony') as the fundamental value shaping the Japanese character. His life and achievements are celebrated at **Horyuji** (Mar–Oct 8am–5pm, Nov–Feb 8am–4.30pm), a large temple complex in southern Nara comprising 40 buildings that became Japan's first Unesco World Heritage Site. Horyuji was actually built decades after Prince Shotoku's death in 622. However, it stands on the site of one of Japan's earliest Buddhist temples, which he built. After entering through the Nandaimon (Great South Gate), walk down another long walkway to the Chumon (Central Gate) and the inner temple grounds. Just past the fearsome Guardian Kings on watch for intruding evil, is the Sai-in, the western compound. This contains Horyuji's five-storey pagoda and the Kondo (main hall), built around 670 and the world's oldest wooden building. Within the To-in (eastern compound) is the octagonal Yumedono (Hall of Dreams), whose exquisite Guze Kannon statue was considered so sacred that it was completely hidden from human eyes from its dedication in 737 until 1884, when it was unwrapped by a visiting American art scholar – with the Meiji government's blessing, of course.

Also in the eastern compound is the Daihozoden (Great Treasure Hall), housing Horyuji's magnificent collection of Buddhist art, among Japan's finest. Included are over 10,000 items, 1,780 of which are classified as national treasures or important cultural assets. Highlights include an Indian-style Shaka triad; the Yumechigae ('Dream Changing') Kannon, said to transform its worshippers' nightmares into pleasant dreams; and the Kudara Kannon, a graceful, willowy statue named after a region in Korea, whose designer and creator was almost certainly Korean. Horyuji was built by craftsmen imported from Korea, and the temple bears much of their distinctive artistic stamp.

Surprisingly, Horyuji also contains a building dedicated to a foreigner: Langdon Warner, a Harvard art professor whom the Japanese have mistakenly credited with saving both Nara and Kyoto from aerial bombing during World War II. The decision to spare them was actually taken by Henry Stimson, the US Secretary of War, who knew the cities from his own pre-war visits.

Osaka

More than just Japan's second city, **Osaka** is also the perfect base from which to explore nearby Nara and Kyoto by train. Although Osaka is overshadowed by Tokyo in the big-city stakes, it is a vibrant and energetic world capital in its own right and certainly has plenty to offer the curious visitor.

Indeed, for many visitors Osaka is more truly 'Japanese' than Tokyo, having a more distinctive flavour and character than its sprawling rival to the east. Osakans pride themselves on being warmer, friendlier and more spontaneous than their Tokyo cousins, whom they love to dismiss as formal and uptight. They are also renowned throughout Japan for two things: doing business and eating.

Here, business and pleasure are inextricably linked – and have been for hundreds of years. The city's commercial reputation reflects its origins as the national merchants' capital and a major trading hub. When Hideyoshi built his main castle in the centre of Osaka after unifying the country in 1583, the city's prosperity seemed written in stone. With an uninhibited merchant class eager to throw its newly acquired wealth around, Osaka quickly became Japan's undisputed entertainment and theatrical centre. Despite the economic slowdown and recession of the 1990s that followed the bursting of Japan's economic bubble, anyone strolling around central Osaka's famous night-time entertain-

A business centre by day, Osaka also thrives at night

ment districts will quickly realise how much its residents love to eat, drink and party. In fact, so dedicated are Osakans to the cult of eating that they are known for *kuidare* (eating until you drop or until you go bankrupt, depending on the interpretation). Osaka will win no urban beauty contests, but there are plenty of sights to see here, including a couple of interesting museums, a remarkable aquarium and an underground shopping complex that might be the world's largest.

The best way to see Osaka is by subway. Taxis are expensive and vulnerable to the city's sticky traffic situation; and information on the tourist-unfriendly bus service is almost entirely in Japanese only. An all-day subway pass (available at any ticket ma-

chine) costs the equivalent of less than four central-area subway tickets (about £12). Osaka has one of the best tourist information networks of any Japanese city. These are dotted all over the city, but the main centre is in Umeda JR. A good place to start exploring is the bustling **Umeda** area, containing Japan Railways Osaka Station, three subway stations and two private railway stations. It also has the most famous department stores outside Tokyo, the gigantic Hankyu and Hanshin buildings (whose private railways serve Kyoto and Kobe). The Osaka City Tourist Information Office is just inside the main entrance to the Hankyu Station. Umeda marks the northern end of the business and entertainment district popularly known as Kita ('North'), and is the essence of modern Osaka's hustle and bustle.

At rush hour, Umeda's teeming subway platforms rival the crowd scenes for which Tokyo's subway is so notorious. Equally impressive crowd scenes occur below Umeda in a mammoth network of shops, bars and cosy inexpensive restaurants whose

The Kimono

Surprisingly, the kimono did not originate in Japan, but, like many things 'distinctly' Japanese, has its roots in China – the Chinese court. During the Nara Period (710–784), the Japanese imperial court adopted the Chinese-style *p'ao*, a long, kimono-like attire brilliant with colours and embellishment; kimono styles used by Japanese women during this time were similar to the *p'ao* garments of women in Tang-dynasty China. Indeed, the Heian-era court dress worn by Japan's emperor and empress today during special occasions displays Chinese characteristics unchanged since the 12th century.

As did most things adopted by the Japanese over the centuries, the kimono underwent changes that eventually made it distinctly Japanese. During the Muromachi Period (1338–1573), for example, women introduced the *obi*, a narrow sash, and adapted the sleeves to fit Japanese climate and styles.

scale boggles the mind. The basement of every large building in a one-mile radius is linked to form a modern commercial labyrinth. It actually comprises several shopping centres seamlessly interconnected to ensure maximum customer and cash turnover. To explore its fascinating subterranean sights, start with the 'Whity Umeda,' under the Hankyu and Hanshin buildings, then move on to 'Herbis Plaza' – but don't expect to see daylight again for some time.

A suitable cure for your extended period underground is to go up – 40 storeys up to the top of **Umeda Sky Building**.

Family photo opportunity

This futuristic and unusual structure is actually two glass-and-steel towers linked at the top, from which the 'Floating Observatory' provides a panoramic view of Osaka city and the surrounding countryside.

Shopping arcades are a staple feature of every Japanese city, town and village. Unsurprisingly, Osaka boasts some of Japan's most impressive – or excessive, depending on your taste. You can spend fascinating hours exploring the covered Hankyu Higashidori arcade near the Hankyu Station, less upmarket but no less fascinating than the more famous Shinsaibashi arcade *(see page 125)*. In the south of Kita, across from the US Consulate, is Kita Shinchi, Osaka's première dining and entertainment quarter, centred around the main street of Shinchi Hondori. This area is great for people-watching, but to eat here it helps to have a generous expense account.

Osaka Castle's main entrance

Near Kyobashi Station is the **Fujita Art Museum**, which has a fine collection of Chinese and Japanese paintings from the 11th century to the present. If you've become an adept of the tea ceremony, you'll appreciate the excellent collection of 14th-century objects: ceramic tea bowls, tea kettles and caddies, as well as bamboo spoons, whisks and flower vases. For more ceramics, stop in at the **Museum of Oriental Ceram-** ics (Tue–Sun 9.30am–5pm; www.moco.org.jp), located in the garden at one end of Nakanoshima, the 'central island' in the middle of the large river running through Osaka's centre. Here you can find fine specimens of the Korean and Chinese ceramics that so strongly influenced Japan's own styles. This is one of the best such collections in the world, with more than 1,000 pieces. Most of Osaka's municipal buildings are on Nakanoshima, including an elegant European-style town hall dating from 1918, one of the few red-brick buildings in Japan.

Here you'll also get a splendid view of **Osaka Castle** (daily 9am–5pm; www.osakacastle.net), which is dramatically illuminated at night. To celebrate his unification of Japan after more than a century of civil war, Hideyoshi had made the castle the country's greatest fortress, so the Tokugawa felt obliged to destroy it in 1615 after snatching power away from Hideyoshi's heir. They later rebuilt it to bolster their own prestige, only to burn it down once again in a fit of pique when the Meiji Restoration of imperial power abolished their shogunate in 1868. Today, a reinforced-concrete replica reproduces only the great five-storeyed tower, 42m (138ft) high, surrounded by moats and ivy-covered ramparts. The castle contains an interesting but disappointingly modern museum displaying armour, weapons, costumes and historical documents. There's also an enchanting collection of *bunraku* puppets – a rare chance to see them at close range.

Providing a welcome touch of green amid all the asphalt, ginkgo and sycamore trees line the impressive Midosuji Boulevard. This thoroughfare runs south from Umeda to Kita's southern counterpart, Minami. On one side of Midosuji is America-mura ('America Village'), the favourite posing ground for Osaka's desperately trendy youth, so named for the large number of stores selling much-sought-after secondhand apparel imported from the US.

One block east of Midosuji is Osaka's famous **Shinsaibashi shopping arcade**, a consumer-frenzy mecca second in national status only to Ginza and Shinjuku in Tokyo. If you have time for only one evening walk in Osaka, this is the one. Although the arcade begins over 1.6km (1 mile) north, start from exit 6 of Shinsaibashi Station on the Midosuji subway line, between the Sogo and Daimaru department stores, and turn right to make your way south. Every night of the week, this entire area is teeming with businessmen frequenting night clubs, hostess bars and private drinking clubs. (Many of these clubs are confusingly called 'snack bars'. But tourists beware! These bizarre establishments are the true home of the £20 glass of beer, with prices aimed squarely at lonely executives with expense

Osaka Castle

Shinsaibashi shopping arcade

accounts looking for a home away from home.) This is where Osaka's trendy youth prowl for action, as do many of Osaka's growing pack of young foreign residents seduced by the lure of easy yen. On Saturday afternoons and evenings, the place is a teeming throng of humanity. Wandering along the side streets at night allows you to soak up the heady atmosphere of pleasure and commerce that has characterised this part of Osaka for centuries.

At the far south is the small Ebisu Bridge known as Hikkake-bashi or 'pick-up bridge', a favourite meeting place for Osaka's trendiest young things. Just before you cross the bridge, on your left is an arch announcing the start of **Soemon-cho**, a colourful street of late-night restaurants and night clubs that is Minami's answer to Kita-Shinchi near Umeda. Note the ultra-modern black-and-chrome Kirin Plaza beer hall next to the entrance to Soemon-cho.

As you cross the bridge, stop in the middle to immerse yourself in the sights and sounds of the people, the blazing neon and the Dotomburi River below you. Hundreds of years ago, in Osaka's heyday as the country's theatre and entertainment capital, the biggest stars would arrive by boat to enter the riverside back entrances of the many theatres on Dotomburi, which is just south of the river. Frenzied fans would pack this very bridge for a glimpse of their idols arriving in ornate medieval waterborne equivalents of the modern stretch limousine.

Turning left on the other side of the bridge brings you to **Dotomburi**, which at night is Osaka's ultimate assault on the senses. A cornucopia of bizarre creatures adorn the buildings flanking this pedestrian mall: giant monsters slither down the buildings, restaurants, cinemas, theatres, games centres and steamy noodle bars. No photograph can capture the intensity of this strange and unforgettable concourse.

At the other end of Dotomburi is the **Nipponbashi** area. This is where you will find Den-Den Town, Osaka's sadly underwhelming answer to Tokyo's Akihabara electronics district. Nipponbashi is also famous as the national home of *bunraku*, Japan's dazzling traditional puppet theatre. Although various forms of puppet theatre date back to the 11th century, the remarkably expressive and elaborately costumed *bunraku* style was thriving by the 17th century in both Osaka and Kyoto. Although its popularity waned during the Meiji period, it has been 'rediscovered' this century, the most dramatic evidence being the vast investment in the **National Bunraku Theatre** in Nipponbashi. *Bunraku* is a Japanese performance art of surprising dramatic intensity, worth seeing if only for an hour or so in the middle of a busy day of sightseeing. Although all dialogue and narration are in Japanese, an English interpretation device or an English programme is always available.

In the neighbouring Namba district, the **Shin-Kabuki-za Theatre** (at the bottom of Midosuji Boulevard) gives *kabuki* performances only three weeks each year. But there's plenty of other traditional drama such as *kyogen* farces and *manzai* comic double-acts. In spring each year, the Osaka International Festival of drama and music takes place both at the theatre and in the Festival Hall on Nakanoshima Island. Even if you don't venture within, the building itself is very dramatic and should not be missed.

Bunraku bard

Many of the most popular heroic and tragic Bunraku dramas were written by Osaka's own Monzaemon Chikamatsu (1653–1724), the playwright the Japanese claim as their own Shakespeare.

Between the Nipponbashi and Namba districts, try to find near-by Doguya-suji, ('Kitchen Street'), a narrow alley of restaurant whole-salers. This is the place to buy souvenirs of all the imitation food you've seen in restaurant windows, together with Japanese-style plates, bowls, glasses, sake sets, lacquerware, giant paper lanterns and a million other things you never expected to see for sale.

South of Namba, between Ebisucho and Tennoji stations, is the Tsutenkaku Tower, a rather desperate imitation of the Eiffel Tower (and perhaps the only structure that makes Kyoto's tower look im-pressive). The view from the observation deck over 90m (300ft) up is panoramic but hardly worth the effort. The nearby **Osaka Municipal Art Museum** (Tue–Sun 9.30am–5pm; http://osaka-art. info-museum.net), near Tennoji Station, is worth visiting for its celebrated Abe Collection of 200 Chinese paintings (9th–13th centuries) and its Ming- and Ching-dynasty ceramics (14th–19th centuries). Also worth visiting, the **Keitakuen garden** (Tue–Sun 9.30am–5pm) is part of Tennoji Park, a large parkland with a huge

These paper lanterns are sold on Doguya-suji

conservatory and greenhouse. A traditional Japanese garden circling a pond, the Keitakuen was donated by the wealthy owner of a trading company, one Baron Sumitomo. The large permanent encampment of homeless people around Tennoji Park makes the area more than a little seedy (but not at all dangerous).

Close by is Osaka's most famous temple, **Shitennoji**, founded in 593 by the revered reforming lawgiver, Prince Shotoku. Unfortunately, the buildings in this large temple are concrete reproductions of the originals destroyed by bombing in World War II. However, the large stone *torii* gateway is the oldest in Japan, dating back to 1294. Shitennoji also hosts Osaka's largest temple market on the 21st of each month, featuring antiques, used clothing and miscellaneous items. Further south is the **Sumiyoshi Taisha** shrine, dedicated to the god of peace, song and seafaring. The shrine's large and attractive arched bridge is just one of the features enjoyed by the three million visitors who come to make prayer offerings on the first three days of the New Year. Although the shrine is thought to have been founded in the 3rd century, the present buildings are relatively recent reproductions.

Osaka Port at the far west of the city offers two ideal distractions for all the family. The futuristic **Kaiyukan Aquarium** (daily 10am–8pm; www.kaiyukan.com) has at its core one of the world's largest indoor tanks, containing a dramatic collection of sharks and other large deep-sea fish. Arranged in a descending spiral around it are other tanks representing the denizens of the Pacific Ocean's seismic 'ring of fire'. The aquarium is set in a large complex of unusual shops and restaurants that also contains the **Suntory Museum** (Tue–Sun 10.30am–7.30pm; www.suntory.com/culture-sports/smt). In addition to regular art exhibitions, this wildly abstract structure features Osaka's IMAX wide-screen theatre. The entire area makes for a great afternoon's break from the pressures of Osaka sightseeing.

Two interesting additions to the city's cultural and entertainment legacy have sprung up in this former bayside wasteland zone. The thought-provoking **Osaka Human Rights Museum** (Tue–Sun

10am–5pm; www.liberty.or.jp), is an astonishing institute to find in Japan, a country that is often accused of being in denial on a number of sensitive historical and social questions. On a lighter note, Osaka's highly successful transplant, **Universal Studios Japan** (daily, hours vary), has all the attractions familiar to those who have visited the original movie theme park, including motion simulation rides such as Jaws, ET Adventure and Jurassic Park.

The nearby **Maishima Incineration Plant** may seem an odd choice for a day's sightseeing, but the building, designed by Austrian artist and architect Friedensreich Hundertwasser, is a marvel to behold. The colourful high-tech burner, resembling a surrealist castle with turrets, tiered gardens and ceramic columns, has to be seen to be believed.

Kobe

Kobe exploded onto the world's headlines with the suddenness of the earthquake that ravaged the city on 17 January 1995, claiming a final death toll of over 6,000. But a combination of remarkable communal solidarity and determination coupled with

Yakuza

Yakuza origins date to the 1600s, when unemployed samurai dressed in odd clothing and carrying longswords sometimes terrorised people for leisure. Later, men called *bakuto* were hired by the shogun to gamble with labourers paid by the government to reclaim some of the substantial wages.

Kobe is the home of the Yamaguchi-gumi, the largest of Japan's dozen or so conglomerate gangs founded in the 1920s. Police estimate there are over 150,000 *yakuza* members in 2,000 gangs affiliated with the conglomerate groups. The *yakuza* have established alliances with Chinese Triads, Mafia in the US and Italy, drug cartels and others. Legitimate businesses mask their criminal activities; it is estimated that *yakuza* have funnelled well over US$10 billion into legitimate investments in the US and Europe.

Kobe beef is famed worldwide for its distinctive, strong flavour

extensive private- and public-sector investment lie behind a re-
covery that is nothing short of astonishing.

Hemmed into a narrow coastal strip between the Rokko Mountains and the Inland Sea, this port city came into its own after
American pressure forced Japan to open up to foreign trade in
1868. The merchants who established a foothold in Kobe included
large numbers of Persians and Indian traders. Today it is still
known within Japan for its small but highly visible foreign business community, some of whose families have called Kobe home
for generations. Kobe is a major cosmopolitan centre with thriving restaurants, bars and nightlife, not to mention Nankin-machi,
Japan's most famous 'Chinatown'.

One early influence of the foreign residents was the development
of the nationally famous Kobe beef in a country that had never
touched the stuff until foreign barbarians began demanding steaks.
Raised nearby in Tajima or Tamba, the cattle produce a uniquely
fatty meat, with a special flavour said to come from a daily dose of
strong beer. The price in the restaurants on Tor Road is exorbitant,

but you might like to try the beef either grilled straight or prepared Japanese-style as *sashimi* (raw), *sukiyaki* (thinly sliced and pan-fried), or *shabu-shabu* (stewed in a hot-pot broth).

Kobe's two main central shopping districts are Sannomiya and neighbouring Motomachi, both with large department stores and fashionable boutiques. Numerous smaller shops are in the Koka-shita arcade, a long but narrow covered shopping passage beneath the railways tracks that is definitely not for the claustrophobic.

Kobe's biggest tourist draw, though, is mainly of interest to domestic Japanese visitors. **Kitano**, the old foreign merchants' residential district, preserves some of the 19th-century European-style houses that survived World War II. For foreign tourists, the most interesting thing about this area will probably be witnessing the fascination these residences hold over Japanese visitors. Kitano's Jain temple, mosque and synagogue add to the exotic appeal of this unusual area.

Not to be missed is Kobe's exciting harbour district, a spacious waterfront area that has been extensively developed since the earthquake. The area, dominated by the futuristic **Kobe Maritime Museum** (Tue–Sun 10am–5pm) and **Port Tower**, is made up of parkland, shopping malls and old red-brick wharves. Kobe's newest feature, **Harbor Land**, a complex of shopping malls, brick-built warehouses, a cinema and a giant Ferris wheel, is across the bay.

Dominating the mountain range that provides Kobe's dramatic backdrop is **Mt Rokko**, which offers a wide range of natural and man-made attractions. To escape the stifling heat of summer, everyone except the super-fit takes the 10-minute cable car ride to the top. Here you will discover a commanding view of Kobe, Osaka, Awaji Island and the Inland Sea. The hiking and cycling trails draw nature-lovers throughout the year.

Behind Mt Rokko is **Arima Onsen**, one of Japan's oldest hot-spring resorts. Like popular hot-spring resorts around the country, this small town has been the site of furious development, and the many small traditional inns *(ryokan)* and bathhouses are now dwarfed by large, ugly concrete hotels. Nevertheless, Arima Onsen still offers an ideal introduction to the pleasures of bathing Japanese-style, whether through a visit of a few hours to one of the large and luxuriously equipped centres, or a night spent in a traditional family-run hot-spring inn.

Ise-Shima

Ise-Shima National Park, southeast of Osaka, is home to the Outer and Inner shrines of Ise. These deceptively simple structures are no less than the sacred repository of the national identity – Shinto sanctuaries dedicated nearly 2,000 years ago to Japan's founding deities. Their atmospheric setting in serene woodland reveals more strongly than anywhere else the profound links between modern Japan and its mythical origins. Be forewarned: for foreign tourists, Ise is not a destination for picturesque sightseeing, and there isn't really very much to see or photograph (especially since taking pictures of the Inner Shrine is forbidden).

The Shinto identity embodied in the shrines of Ise is quite distinct from Japan's other man-made institutions. Nature itself is the

Rocks off the Ise peninsula

primal essence enshrined and worshipped at Ise, as implied by the carefully orchestrated approach to the sanctuaries past the limpid Isuzu River and through the forest. Although the sacred structures represent the ultimate focus of the Shinto religion, they are dismantled and renewed every 20 years – one of the most explicit manifestations of the traditional Japanese belief in transience and perpetual renewal.

Both the Inner and Outer shrines comprise a main hall and two treasure houses, each enclosed within four fences. Only members of the imperial family and high-ranking priests are allowed past the second of the four fences. This restriction reinforces the notion of the imperial family as living descendents and representatives of the gods – despite the emperor's renunciation of divinity announced as one of the terms of surrender at the end of World War II (when some people fainted upon hearing the emperor's voice on the radio for the first time).

The shrines are most easily reached from Nagoya via the Kintetsu Railway to Uji-Yamada Station. In addition to the famous shrines, you can explore more of this attractively scenic peninsula, with its national park, the haunting image of the sacred 'wedded rocks' at Futamigaura beach and the resort town of Kashikojima at the southern end of the Kintetsu railway's Shima line.

The Outer Shrine

A short walk from Uji-Yamada Station is **Geku**, the Outer Shrine. It is dedicated to the God of the Earth, who was sent down to Japan by the Sun Goddess Amaterasu. Originally situated near present-day Kyoto, the shrine was moved here in 478. The main entrance takes you to the first sacred gateway (torii), which in Japan always symbolises the threshold of holy ground. Both shrines' surprisingly primitive

Ritual cleansing

Concern for ritual purification requires that Japanese pilgrims rinse their mouths at a water trough when approaching a shrine. Priests also wave sacred branches over the faithful.

design is thought to be based on those of granaries and store-houses from prehistoric times.

As you walk along the avenue of pines and giant cedars, you pass on the right the An-zaisho, the emperor's rest house, and Sanshujo, the rest house for the imperial family. Beyond a second *torii* is the Kaguraden, Hall of the Sacred Dances. In return for a donation to the shrine, the shrine maidens *(miko)*, dressed in the typically Shinto outfit of bright-red pleated skirts with white blouses, will perform one of the dances. The girls wield branches of the holy *sakaki* tree and dance to an orchestra composed of wooden clappers *(hyoshigi)*, plucked zither *(koto)*, mouth organ *(sho)* and the oboe-like *hichiriki*, to-gether with flute and drum.

Shinto shrines reflect key elements of the national identity

The avenue comes to an end at the Geku's Shoden (main shrine building), which – together with its eastern and western treasure houses – is enclosed by a series of four unvarnished wooden fences. This is where Shinto priests in white robes with black belts and black lacquered clogs stand to bless worshippers as they make a silent obeisance. The Shoden itself is just 6m (20ft) high, a little less in width, and 10m (33ft) long. Each shrine is constructed of plain, unadorned Japanese cypress wood, brought especially from the Kiso Mountains in the Central Alps, northeast of Nagoya. The style of the cross-beamed roofs and simple wooden frames is the same as that used more than 2,000 years ago, before Chinese architecture exerted its influence when Buddhism arrived here from Korea. This is a special style of Shinto architecture that is prohibited from being used at other shrines.

The **Geku-Jin-en Sacred Park**, at the foot of Mt Takakura, is an integral part of the sanctuary. The walk to the inner shrine takes you along a picturesque tree-shaded avenue lined with stone lanterns.

The Inner Shrine

The **Naiku** (Inner Shrine) is the more important of the two shrines, as it is dedicated to Amaterasu, the Sun Goddess and supreme deity of Shinto. The Naiku holds the sacred eight-pointed mirror *(yata-no-kagami)*, which is one of the three treasures of the imperial throne. The Naiku's layout and the construction of its Shoden are similar to those of the Geku, although the approach to the Naiku over the Uji Bridge across the Isuzu River is more picturesque. Like the shrines, the bridge is renewed every two decades.

Shinto priests perform rituals at Ise-Shima

The ritual dismantling of the shrines every 20 years (known as *sengu-shiki*) goes back to prehistoric times, when sacred structures tended to be erected for special ceremonies rather than as permanent places of worship. You will notice beside each shrine an area of open ground on which the new shrine is to be erected – in 2013 – in identical form. The structures are broken up into small pieces and distributed to the faithful as talismans. The whole process is both painstaking and expensive, and the 'democratisation' of the imperial institutions since the emperor renounced his divinity means the shrines (rather than the state) must now foot the bill. To defray costs, worshippers must make a generous donation to receive a piece of the old shrine.

Sacred treasures

The Three Sacred Treasures of the imperial throne are the sacred mirror, held at the Naiku; the sword, which resides at the Atsuta Shrine in Nagoya; and the jewel, kept in the Imperial Palace in Tokyo.

You can join the Japanese visitors down at the Isuzu River, where they perform a rite of purification by washing their mouths with its clear, fresh waters. At the same time, they play with the fat red, silver and black carp swimming around nearby.

West of the shrines by Sangu-line train, Toba is famous for **Mikimoto Pearl Island** (daily Jan–Nov 8.30am–5pm, Dec 9am–4.30pm; www.mikimoto-pearl-museum.co.jp), the home of cultured pearls. The museum here has displays explaining the process, and you can watch female divers collecting sea urchins, abalone and seaweed from the nearby pearl rafts.

Wakayama

South of Osaka is **Wakayama**, a large prefecture whose long coastline and lush greenery have long been a magnet for domestic tourists. In addition to hundreds of temples, shrines and hot-spring resorts, Wakayama features some of the country's most popular beaches. Further south is **Koyasan**, the centre of the Shingon branch of esoteric Buddhism, one of Japan's most important religious

Mizumejizo-san statues on display at Okunoin

enclaves and, since 2004, a Unesco World Heritage Site. Now comprising over 120 temple buildings as well as numerous shrines, pagodas and stupas, this large religious settlement is located at the top of Mt Koya, a 1,006m (3,300ft) peak. Koyasan was already known as a sacred site for ascetic practices when Kobo Daishi, a revered Buddhist priest, teacher and scholar, received imperial permission to establish a religious community to develop his new Shingon sect in 816.

The mausoleum of the *kukai* ('great teacher,' as he is known) is located at the deepest reaches of **Okunoin**, Japan's most famous cemetery and one of Koyasan's biggest draws. Once the *kukai* was buried there, the great and the humble alike were quick to see the merit of a final resting place near him. The graves of hundreds of thousands from all walks of life now occupy the site, with the remains of emperors, warlords, warriors, samurai and poets all jostling for space. Their tombs and stone markers range from the ostentatious to the elegant, the well preserved to the decrepit.

Kongobuji, one of the many temples here, contains valuable Momoyama-period screens, but the real attraction is the Banryutei, the largest stone garden in Japan. The huge granite rocks, set in white sand, symbolise two dragons in a sea of cloud.

Well over a million ancestor-worshipping Japanese descend on Koyasan and Okunoin on major public holidays, especially those commemorating the dead. If you are wise enough to avoid these times, consider spending the night in one of some 60 temple lodgings *(shukubo)* that offer surprisingly comfortable traditional accommodation to visitors and travellers. The main highlight of a stay at one of these special temples is the chance to sample the luxurious Buddhist vegetarian temple cuisine *(shojin-ryori)* served only in such lodgings. The path to enlightenment can be surprisingly pleasurable.

CHUBU

The central region of Honshu (Japan's main island), **Chubu** stretches northeast from Kansai across the Hida, Kiso and Akaishi mountains – known collectively as the Japan Alps – to the plains of the north coast and the Sea of Japan. It's most easily explored in an excursion from the Kansai region by train in a picturesque mountain-railway journey from Nagoya. You can visit the lovely town of Takayama, set in the midst of imposing mountain scenery, and the historic coastal city of Kanazawa.

Takayama

The Takayama-line train, from Nagoya via Gifu, takes you along the Kiso and Hida river valleys. The leisurely three-hour journey passes through steep gorges, narrow terraced rice paddies and neatly tailored tea plantations, with not a square centimetre of usable land wasted. The train stops by riverside markets where farmers trade fruit, vegetables and gossip with passengers.

Takayama is a town famous for its carpenters – a reputation

Sunset over the Akaishi mountain, or Japan Alps, in Chubu

going back to the great days of the imperial courts of Nara and Kyoto. With the harvests of its Hida mountain district too meagre to contribute taxes to the national treasury, the town sent instead its skilful artisans *(Hida no takumi)* to help build the temples and palaces of the imperial capital. Those skills have been handed down to present-day craftsmen working in yew wood, and the old timbered houses are exquisitely maintained in traditional style. The local lord in turn borrowed the capital's grid pattern when laying out medieval Takayama, which became known as 'Little Kyoto'.

Takayama is a good place to try out family-style guesthouses *(minshuku; see page 221)* – they're especially friendly here. You can get around on foot, although renting a bicycle at the railway station will give you easy access to the surrounding countryside.

Start your day at the open-air Asaichi morning market down on the east bank of the Miya River, north of Yasugawa Street bridge. Savour the clear mountain air as you enjoy the display of

Elderly Takayama resident

fruit and vegetables from Hida farms and the flowers and nuts brought down from the hills.

A little way back from the river, heading south, you'll find the delightful old houses and workshops of Kami-Sannomachi and Furuimachinami streets. The high-quality craftwork here, woodcarvings, lacquerware and pottery, is renowned throughout Japan. Furuimachinami is quieter and more residential, with long, two-storey, unpainted dark timber houses, lattice façades and low-balconied verandahs, plus a few flowers and shrubs in pots or *hako-niwa* box gardens to add some colour. Some of the old houses have been redeveloped as museums and eclectic galleries.

Just east of the riverside market are two merchants' houses, Yoshijima-ke and Kusakabe Mingeikan, the latter turned into a superb folkcraft museum displaying local costumes, woodcarvings and the fine, transparent lacquerware *(shunkeinuri)* that highlights rather than conceals the grain of the wood.

Takayama's most important temple is 16th-century **Kokubunji**. Next to the three-storey pagoda is a ginkgo tree said to be over 1,200 years old. Southeast of the town is Shiroyama Park, whose unlandscaped slopes covered with wild flowers have a pleasantly natural look and offer an extensive panorama of the town and the Japan Alps beyond.

Hida Minzoku-mura (daily 8.30am–5pm) is a fascinating open-air museum of authentic old farmhouses from the region, most of them rescued from an area flooded by nearby Mihoro Dam. Laid out in an attractive hillside setting 800m (½ mile) southwest of Takayama Station, the houses – many of them three or four storeys high, with steeply pitched grass-thatch roofs – are oddly reminiscent of those in European Alpine villages. The houses display old farm tools and cooking utensils, and some operate as workshops where you can watch the much-vaunted local craftsmen demonstrating their skills in lacquerwork, carving, weaving and dyeing.

A more authentic showcase for local architecture, especially the steep, thatch-roofed, A-framed farm houses known as gassho-zukuri ('praying hands'), can be seen in the villages of **Shirakawa-**

go northwest of Takayama. Surrounded by mountains and forest, this well-preserved group of interconnecting villages and valleys was declared a Unesco World Heritage Site in 1995. Try to avoid visiting at weekends, which are deservedly crowded.

Some 60km (40 miles) south of Shirakawa-go is the beautiful hill town of **Gujo-Hachiman**. Gujo sits at the confluence of two rivers, the Nagara and the Yoshino, in a valley that was once a waystation on an important trade route leading to the Sea of Japan. The crystal clear, pebble-strewn rivers are alive with *ayu* (sweetfish) and *satsuki masu*, a type of trout unique to these waters. The town consists of dark, stained wood homes and shops, white plastered buildings, wooden bridges, steep walls made from boulders, and narrow stone-paved lanes, along which museums, galleries and attractive shops selling local products like Tsumugi textiles can be found. The town is famous for its extraordinary month-long Gujo Odori, or 'Gujo Dance', held at the height of O-Bon, the Festival of the Dead, in August. The castle, at the summit of a steep hill, is the best place from which to appreciate the shape of the town, which resembles that of a fish.

Flower-bedecked terrace in a traditional Chubu village

Kanazawa

The largest city in northern Chubu, **Kanazawa** has been able to preserve its older charms from the assaults of the Tokugawa shoguns and the bombs of World War II by pursuing a peaceful career of arts, crafts and scholarship. It is home to a major university as well as an arts and crafts college. Kanazawa is still considered an archetypal castle town, even though the university now occupies the spot once dominated by the

Kenrokuen is a classical Edo-period 'strolling' garden

long-destroyed castle. Still, there are some very pleasant walks around what are still referred to as the castle grounds.

Kenrokuen Park, a classical Edo-period 'strolling' garden regarded as one of the three best in Japan, is a good place to start your visit. The park has a plethora of ponds spanned by elegant stone bridges, together with stone lanterns, waterfalls, serpentine streams, cherry trees and pines. Artfully constructed hillocks provide panoramic views of the landscaping. The central Kasumigaike (Misty Lake) is the most attractive of the ponds, graced by its Tortoise Shell Island – the tortoise being much favoured by the Japanese as a symbol of long life.

Among Kanazawa's other specialities is its pretty, five-colour glazed *kutani* pottery, which you'll see in many town-centre shops. If you're interested enough to make a small investment, first look at the marvellous samples in the Municipal Art Museum in the park before buying. West of the park is Nagamachi, the old samurai quarter. Wander freely along the secluded canals past the dark timbered houses, all situated in very narrow, zigzagging streets to hamper enemy attack. The superb **Saihitsu-an** house features silk-dyers creating unbelievably expensive material for kimono. On the eastern edge of town, north of the Umeno Hashi bridge across the Asano River, is the old geisha district, slightly more rundown than Nagamachi but no less quaint.

WESTERN HONSHU AND SHIKOKU

The area around the Inland Sea offers a wide range of attractions, from the varied towns and cities of Western Honshu to the major pilgrimage destination of Shikoku.

Himeji

The small industrial city of Himeji is dominated by the marvellous snow-white castle that seems to hover above the town. Variously called the White Egret or Heron castle, **Himeji Castle** (daily June–Aug 9am–5pm, Sept–May 9am–4pm; www.himeji-castle.gr.jp) is a

Himeji, the only castle in Japan still preserved in its original form

15-minute stroll from the *shin-kansen* station along a road lined with modern sculptures. Resting resplendent on the banks of the Senba-gawa, the castle of Himeji is the largest and most elegant of the dozen existing medieval castles in Japan – and the only one preserved in its original form. Although the city was extensively bombed during World War II, the castle emerged unscathed. The splendid building dates from the early 1600s. When the famous unifiers Nobunaga, Hideyoshi and Tokugawa fought

Stepping stones in Koko-en

to end the 16th-century civil wars, Hideyoshi used Himeji as a base of operations against the recalcitrant warlords of Western Honshu. Although much of the castle's interior seems dark and austere, this highlights the magnificent wood floors and panelling and the superb joinery and construction techniques.

A special combination ticket is available for both Himeji Castle and nearby **Koko-en** (May–Aug 9am–6pm, Sept–Apr 9am–5pm), a superb landscaped garden built in 1992 by a Kyoto-based master gardener on the site of a former samurai residence. Koko-en actually comprises nine distinct gardens, each with a special theme such as bamboo, pine trees, seedlings, summer trees and flowers. Don't miss the tea ceremony garden, carefully designed to be appreciated from the traditional Urasenke-style teahouse, where visitors (and especially foreign tourists) are invited to relax on *tatami* mats and enjoy a bowl of strong green tea and a sweet ceremoniously served by elegant kimono-clad tea ceremony students. (When served your bowl of tea, don't forget to bow slowly and turn the tea bowl three times before sipping the frothy brew.)

Kurashiki

Surrounded by heavily industrialised suburbs, the old centre of **Kurashiki** has canals lined with dreamy willow trees – a reverse comment on the horrors of war. This is practically the only town of any consequence here along the Inland Sea coast to have emerged unscathed from the terrible fire-bombings of 1945. It thus provides an all-too-rare glimpse of provincial life in prewar Japan. In the era of the Tokugawa shoguns, the canals were used to carry rice and grain in barges for onward shipment to the great markets of Osaka and Edo. The elegant black-brick granaries have been beautifully preserved to house the town's many museums of art, folkcrafts and archaeology. You'll certainly find a day's visit to Kurashiki a very welcome change from the relentless modernity of some of the cities nearby.

The old part of town is best explored on foot. There are half a dozen museums tucked into an elbow of the canal, but not all of them are worth seeing. Be sure to note down the Japanese names of the better ones before setting out.

One of the most delightful is the **Kurashiki Mingeikan** folk art museum (Tue–Sun 9am–5pm, Dec–Feb until 4.15pm), displaying not only Japanese, Korean and Chinese pottery, glassware, textiles

Other Museums in Kurashiki

In 1930 Ohara Magosaburo built the nation's first museum of Western art, the **Ohara Museum of Art** (Tue–Sun 9am–5pm; www.ohara.or.jp), and stocked it with works by El Greco, Monet, Matisse, Renoir, Gauguin, and Picasso. The neo-classical building remains the city's centrepiece, although new galleries have proliferated around it over the years. Other rooms are devoted to the works of the great *mingei* (Japanese folk art) potters such as Hamada Shoji, Kawai Kanjiro and Tomimoto Kenkichi.

The first floor of the **Japanese Folk Toy Museum** (daily 9am–5pm) is packed with traditional Japanese toys, dolls and kites, while a collection of toys from around the world can be seen on the second floor. The adjacent toy shop is as interesting as the museum.

and bamboo-ware, but also Native American and European peasant ceramics and basketry with which to compare the Asian art. The Ohara Tokikan pottery hall is devoted to the work of modern pottery masters Kanjiro Kawai, Shoji Hamada and Kenkichi Tomimoto, as well as their much admired friend, Bernard Leach, the influential British potter credited with popularising Japanese rustic ceramic styles and techniques abroad.

At the **Kurashiki Ninagawa Museum of Art** (daily 9am–5pm), the outside world is very much the focus of the Ninagawa family's collection of ancient Greek, Egyptian, Roman and Persian ceramics, sculpture

Cherry tree in bloom

and mosaics, plus 19th-century French and Italian marble and bronze sculptures. There is also some astonishing Rococo porcelain from Meissen, Vienna, Berlin and Sèvres.

Some 45 minutes from Kurashiki on the JR Habuki line, **Bitchu-Takahashi** is a provincial town with a mountain and valley setting whose cultural credentials are second to none. **Raikyu-ji**, a Zen temple that was rebuilt in 1339, has an exquisite dry landscape garden designed by Kobori Enshu. Mount Atago can be glimpsed in the distance and forms the classic 'borrowed view' frequently incorporated into garden designs. The town's well-appointed castle is Japan's highest, constructed at 430m (1,400ft) on the peak of Mount Gagyuzan.

Connoisseurs of large 'strolling' gardens consider the 18th-century **Korakuen**, in the nearby town of Okayama, a must (daily

7.30am–6pm). The Japanese have adopted the traditional Chinese practice of ranking sights and places, and Korakuen is 'officially' one of Japan's three greatest gardens. At the garden's famous tea pavilion you can sample a tea ceremony while contemplating the cherry and plum trees on one side in the spring or the blazing maples on the other in autumn. Across the Asahi River, you can see the ruins of **Okayama Castle**, unusually painted black and called Ujo ('The Crow') in deliberate contrast to Himeji's 'White Heron Castle'.

Hiroshima

Your first reaction as the train pulls into Hiroshima Station might well be surprise. After all, the very name 'Hiroshima' has become

Children's memorial in the Peace Park

a modern metaphor, the ultimate symbol of total obliteration. Yet around the station you see tower blocks, neon signs, cars zipping along the highway – all the signs of a normal town. In fact, modern **Hiroshima** is a city of broad avenues, green parks and almost a million citizens, which is more than double its World War II population.

You might find yourself looking at an old man or woman, guessing how old they were on 6 August 1945 and trying to imagine what they were doing at 8.15am, the instant of the atomic explosion that reverberated around the world. The movingly simple **Peace Memorial Museum** (daily, Aug 8.30am–7pm, Mar–July, Sept–Nov 8.30am–6pm, Dec–Feb

8.30am–5pm) documents the horror with charts, models, photographs, videos, everyday objects transformed by the unimaginable heat of the blast and a life-sized diorama portraying horribly burned victims. One of the most powerful exhibits is a single photograph: a human shadow left imprinted on the steps of the Sumitomo Bank at the moment of the 'flash'. The curators have gone to considerable lengths to document the horror of atomic

Hiroshima by tram

One of the best ways to see Hiroshima's sights is to take a tram. The trams also have historic value. When other Japanese cities and towns dismantled their tram networks after World War II, the tramcars were sent to Hiroshima. Over the years, the city thus acquired an eclectic collection of trams, mostly dating back to the 1940s.

weapons and nuclear war in general, driving towards the inevitable conclusion that such weapons must never again be used.

Outside the museum, the **Cenotaph** contains the names of the 108,956 casualties, with the inscription: 'Let all the souls here rest in peace, for the evil shall not be repeated'. There is also a huge bronze Peace Bell. At the northern end of the park stands the lone structure preserved since 1945: the former Hiroshima Prefectural Industrial Promotion Hall, now known as the 'A-Bomb Dome'. After visiting the emotionally powerful museum, you may wish to seek a therapeutic antidote in the lively shopping centres east of the park around Hondori, Hachobori and Kamiya-cho. But the ultimate venue to restore the spirit is tranquil Miyajima, just 30 minutes away.

Miyajima

Also known as Itsukushima after its celebrated waterfront shrine, **Miyajima** island is one of Japan's most popular travel destinations. Make a very early start to beat the crowds. (It takes about 25 minutes from Hiroshima to Miyajima-guchi Station via Japan Railways, and then 10 minutes by ferry to the island.)

Even if you feel you've seen enough Japanese temples, you will certainly be moved by the striking beauty of the bright red camphorwood arch of **Itsukushima Shrine** rising 16m (52ft) out of the sea in front of the low, brilliant vermilion buildings, themselves raised above the water by stilts. Founded as far back as the 6th century, the shrine is so sacred that, until the fresh wind of reforms instituted during the Meiji era beginning 1868, pregnant women and the seriously ill were carried to the mainland to ensure that no births or deaths would occur on the island. Mourners had to undergo 50 days of purification before being allowed back on Miyajima. While most such religious laws have been relaxed, burials are still not permitted here. Much of Miyajima was destroyed by typhoons in 2004; what you see today is the result of rebuilding in 2005.

Miyajima manages to be both solemn and lively. Sacred *bugaku* and *kagura* dances are performed at the shrine, while numerous souvenir shops do a roaring trade in the local specialities: woodcarvings, both sacred and utterly pornographic, and maple-leaf-shaped sweet buns *(momiji)*. Although most people take the ropeway, the easily negotiable trail leading to the top of 530m (1,739ft) **Mt Misen** is an invigorating hike. The forest is lush and, past the secluded Gumonjido Buddhist temple, the view from the top over the Inland Sea to Hiroshima is a fine reward.

Itsukushima Shrine was founded in the 6th century

Shikoku

Shikoku, the fourth-largest island in Japan and, environmentally, one of the country's least traumatised places, was until recent years a mystical backwater associated with esoteric Buddhism. Shikoku's isolation, both physically and psychologically, changed for ever in 1988 with the completion of the **Seto**

Group photo at Miyajima

Ohashi Bridge, which carries both cars and trains from Honshu, near Kurashiki, to Sakaide on Shikoku. While the jury is still out on whether this was such a good idea after all, it has made this intriguing island accessible to the mainland traveller, and to the thousands of visitors who undertake the island's famous pilgrimage, a circuit of 88 temples associated with the renowned priest Kobo Daishi.

Despite being **Shikoku** island's largest town, **Matsuyama** is a laid-back place, mainly serving as the shopping centre for tourists visiting the hot springs situated 4km (2½ miles) away. **Dogo Spa** is a great place to try out a public bathhouse: don your cotton kimono and clogs, too (if you can manage them). The spring water is alkaline and crystal clear, and good for stomach ailments, the lungs and the nervous system. Pleasingly unlandscaped, **Shiroyama Park** covers the lovely wooded slopes of Katsuyama Hill. It is dominated by the well-preserved **Matsuyama Castle**, which was once the redoubt of the Matsudaira *daimyo*. This most faithful lieutenant of the Tokugawa clan distinguished himself by planting the cedar forest around the shoguns' mausoleums at Nikko.

Just 1.6km (1 mile) from Dogo Spa is the 14th-century **Ishiteji** temple, one of the 88 stages of the springtime Buddhist pilgrimage around Shikoku defined by Kobo Daishi, founder of Shingon esoteric Buddhism. Notice the especially handsome Niomon Gate.

Thousands of pilgrims descend on **Kotohira-gu**, also known as the Kompira-san, every year. People visit this important shrine located halfway up the wooded slopes of Mt Zozusan to pay homage to Omono-Nushi-no-Mikoto, patron saint of voyagers and sea-farers. The ascent along paths lined with stone lanterns and memorial tablets is rewarded with splendid views of the hilly countryside and, on fine days, the distant Inland Sea from the shrine's viewing platforms. A walk to the top of the 785 stairs and back takes at least an hour.

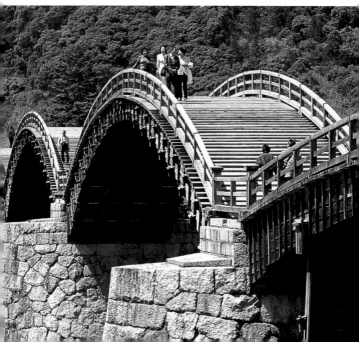

On the northern coastline of the island, **Takamatsu** is a pleasant port city and the gateway to Inland Sea islands like Shodo-shima and Nao-shima. It has an open-air museum of traditional homes called Shikoku Mura, but the main attraction is **Ritsurin Park**, completed in 1745. With its hundreds of pine trees, a pond, a teahouse and elegant wooden bridges, it is one of the finest strolling gardens in Japan.

Visitors can proceed east from here to **Tokushima**, with its famous summer dance festival, the Awa Odori, the whirlpools and craft shops of nearby Naruto, take the ropeway up to Mount Bizan, attend a performance of the town's historic Awa Jurobe Yashiki puppet troupe, or continue south to **Kochi**. An attractive city surrounded by hills to the north and east, Kochi's wide boulevards lined with phoenix

palms, its shopping arcades, imposing castle, shallow rivers, endearingly old-fashioned tramcar system, summer festivals and 300-year-old Sunday market give the city a lively and cultured air.

The port of **Uwajima** on the south-west coast is known for *togyu*, a form of bull-fighting also found in parts of Kyushu and Okinawa, in which the animals lock horns in a battle resembling sumo wrestling. Uwajima's best-known site, however, is **Taga-jinga**, a fertility shrine with a curious **sex museum** chock-a-block with all manner of suggestive offerings in the form of statuary, dolls, erotic literature and art objects. The museum has the reputation for prompting embarrassed giggles and furtive titillation from the Japanese tour groups that visit.

The wooden bridge at Iwakuni was built without a single nail

KYUSHU

Lying the furthest southwest of Japan's four main islands, **Kyushu** has always set itself apart from the others. Its climate is distinctly Mediterranean and even subtropical at its southern tip, and its inhabitants are known for being friendlier, more open and even more 'Westernised' than their compatriots in the rest of the country. Kyushu is also the most volcanic of Japan's islands, famous for its flourishing hot-spring resorts and several active volcanoes. It is a terrific place to explore if you have the time. If you can afford the 'bullet train' just once, this is your chance, as – in one exhilarating sweep – you pass through almost all the major cities of Central and Western Honshu on the way.

Easily accessible from the Asian mainland via Korea, Kyushu has a longer history of significant contacts with foreigners than any other part of Japan. This was especially the case after it found

A Humble People

The Japanese are known for their humility and their politeness. Interpersonal relationships are still largely driven by a constant desire to achieve consensus and avoid disagreement and confrontation.

In Japan's rigidly structured hierarchical society, people's relative status needs to be established at the outset of any interaction. Exchanging business cards is an important preliminary to any meeting or discussion.

However, when dealing with foreigners, the Japanese instinct for warm hospitality usually comes to the fore. People are expected to adopt an outward appearance of humility, which often results in self-deprecating comments with regard to the economy, the diminutive size of houses or inflated prices. Resist the temptation to join in the apparently masochistic highlighting of Japan's shortcomings: disagree politely and find something to praise. The same applies if you are invited to dine in a Japanese home and the arrival of your meal is accompanied by a standard apology regarding the poor quality of the food.

The gentle landscape of a paddyfield, Kyushu

itself on the southern route taken by European merchants and missionaries of the 16th century. Indeed, the famous port city of Nagasaki served as Japan's sole point of contact with the outside world during 260 years of self-imposed isolation.

Kyushu enjoys its special place in the national mythology as the cradle of Japanese civilisation, despite the support of only a meagre amount of archaeological evidence. Legend tells of the Sun Goddess Amaterasu sending her grandson to Mt Takachiho in central Kyushu, armed with the imperial mirror, sword and jewel that Jimmu (Japan's first emperor) used on his conquest of the Yamato Plain near Nara. Modern historians' version is rather less exotic: Jimmu was probably a pirate from Okinawa who settled in Kyushu before launching his campaign to conquer Honshu.

The island's next important historical encounter was with the Mongols under Kublai Khan, when Kyushu was the target of abortive assaults in 1274 and 1281. The islanders' heroic resistance – admittedly on the latter occasion abetted by a timely typhoon *(kamikaze:* 'divine wind'), which sent most of the invading fleet to the bottom

➤

Chariot race

The festival of Hakata Yamagasa takes place in July at Fukuoka. Seven enormous chariots, each weighing over a tonne, are put on show in the town over a period of two weeks. On 15 July, groups of men race the chariots through the town's streets, amid an explosion of noise and general hilarity.

of the sea – earned them a formidable martial reputation. The island proved to be the last bastion of the samurai ideal, when disenfranchised warriors launched the doomed Satsuma Rebellion in their desperation to forestall the relentless march of progress. It was in Kagoshima that the Imperial Japanese Navy was created from the nucleus of ships bought from the British at the end of the 19th century.

Portuguese merchants arrived in Kagoshima in 1543, with the missionaries of St Francis Xavier following close behind. In addition to becoming a centre of Western trade, Nagasaki provided a firm foothold in Japan for the Catholic Church – today much revived after 250 years of brutal suppression under the Tokugawa shoguns.

Northern Kyushu

A lively city of 1.3 million people with mountains to one side and a calm bay on the other, **Fukuoka** styles itself as Japan's gateway to Asia, boasting Kyushu's largest entertainment quarter, an international airport and a bullet-train terminus.

The city is famous for experimental architecture. One of the landmark sites is the **ACROS Fukuoka Building**, a cultural centre with shops, exhibition spaces and a symphony hall. Crowned by a curious tiered mass of greenery called the Step Garden, it stands in a corner of Tenjin's Chuo Park looking like a huge Inca ruin. The **Fukuoka City Public Library**, with its sand-coloured block towers and lozenge-shaped windows, seems of vaguely Yemeni provenance. **Fukuoka Dome**, part of the seafront **Hawks Town** complex, is the largest baseball venue in Japan, and the only one to have a retractable roof. It also boasts one of the longest bars in the world.

Adding to these projects is Momochi, a waterfront complex set to steal the show once it is completed. Fukuoka Tower, a communications tower with an observation deck at a height of 123m (403ft), dominates the reclaimed edges of Momochi. A little south of Fukuoka Tower lies the highly original **Saibu Gas Museum**, a combined science and art venue containing the Gallery of Flame, an otherworldly collection of art objects created with natural gas.

Fukuoka's modernity and willingness to experiment is exemplified by the **Canal City** shopping and entertainment complex, created by Californian architect Jon Jerde. Curvaceous walls with overhanging plants overlook an artificial canal, or 'spouting walkway', with outdoor retail booths and a performance space. You'll find sleek cafés, restaurants, and a number of imported-clothing shops here.

Beppu's hot springs pull in hordes of visitors

On a more traditional note, look out for the town's delicately crafted Hakataningyo dolls, and the famed outdoor food stalls *(yatai)* found throughout the city, which serve the local speciality, *tonkotsu ramen*: a pork and noodle soup.

The first stop on Kyushu's east coast is **Beppu** – perhaps the busiest and certainly the most intense spa town in Japan, with a permanent population of just 125,000 but about nine million visitors a year. The Beppu district boasts eight different hot-spring areas, each with different properties. These include a hot waterfall at the Shibaseki spring, hot sand at Takegawara, hot mud at Kannawa and picturesque outdoor baths in hot ponds among the rocks of the aptly named Hotta Hot Springs.

Beppu's most popular attractions are the open-air 'hell ponds' around Kannawa, which are alternately hilarious and dramatic. In the open-air Umi Jigoku ('Ocean Hell') you can buy eggs hard-boiled in a basket. In Oniyama Jigoku ('Devil's Mountain Hell'), a hundred crocodiles enjoy a hot soak. Chinoike Jigoku ('Blood Pool Hell') is a steaming pond turned blood-red by its iron oxide. At the northern edge of the district is Bozu Jigoku ('Monk's Hell'), an obscenely bubbling mud pond where a Buddhist temple once stood until it was submerged in an earthquake back in the 15th century.

If heat is your thing, pay a visit to the grand old Meiji-era Takegawara public baths, not far from the JR train station. The old wooden building is simply magnificent, although its hot bath is one

Ceramic Cities

When Ri Simpei, an ordinary Korean potter, first chanced upon *kaolin* clay – the essential ingredient for producing fine porcelain – in **Arita** 50km (30 miles) west of Fukuoka around the turn of the 17th century, he probably had little notion of the ramifications of his discovery.

Nearly 400 years later, Arita and its neighbours **Karatsu** and **Imari** are the hub of a thriving pottery industry. The delicate craftsmanship and brightly coloured glazes that are the hallmarks of pottery from this region are prized all over Japan, and further afield, too. Simpei and the other potters who were brought over from Korea as prisoners of the Nabeshima daimyo were kept under close guard so their trade secrets did not slip out.

To understand something about those times, the Nabeshima Hanyo-koen at Okawachiyama (a short bus ride from Imari) portrays the sort of techniques and living conditions that Simpei and his fellow workers lived in. There are plenty of working potteries in the area as well, but the **Kyushu Ceramic Museum** in Arita is the best place to view the full range of Kyushu pottery. Imaizumi Imaemon and Sakaida Kakiemon are celebrated workshops with galleries and shops open to the public.

of the most basic you're likely to encounter. Lie down and have hot sand raked over you by a grinning, grandmotherly attendant – a 10-minute ordeal you'll never forget. The entrance fee allows you to sample all the baths here.

A woman from Kyushu in traditional headwear

One unusual attraction not mentioned in the official tourist literature is Beppu's 'sex museum', which is famous throughout Japan. There are several such collections in Japan, consisting of bizarre images, sculptures and elaborate dioramas depicting many of the darker aspects of human sexuality, often with fantasies involving demons and monsters perpetrating unspeakable deeds upon helpless mortals. This is another 'only in Japan' experience, one definitely not for the faint-hearted.

For a more contemporary experience of Beppu, take the lift to the observation deck of the super-modern, titanium-clad **Global Tower** with its sweeping views of the city.

To the west, the rural village of **Yufuin** has a very different feel from commercialised Beppu. It is relaxed, gentle and charming, featuring old-fashioned farmhouses around tiny Kinrinko Lake. Set at the foot of Mt Yufu – an extinct volcano covered by dense bamboo forest – Yufuin is famous for its hot-spring baths, most of which you can try for just a few hundred yen. The helpful tourist information desk in the JR station can direct you to the most popular or unusual spots, especially those with outdoor baths *(rotenburo)*.

The excellent **Folk Craft Museum** (daily 9am–5.30pm), in an old manor house 20 minutes' walk from the station, holds regular demonstrations of local arts and crafts. Hard-core seekers of local culture will find a single day insufficient for visiting Yufuin's Museum of Modern Art (daily 9am–6pm), the unexpected **Marc Chagall Museum** (daily 9am–5pm) and 15 other art galleries. The gentle paths along the small rivers that meander through the town provide serene views of ricefields and superb scenery.

Further south, the thick groves of palm trees lining the coast at **Miyazaki** serve as a reminder of its position on the edge of the tropics. This resort town has a long and usually uncrowded sandy beach, and there are several pleasant golf courses among the palm trees. **Heiwadai Park** brings together the prehistoric past and the frequently strange present. The park's prefectural museum (Tue–Sun 9am–4.30pm) displays some small clay figures *(haniwa)* unearthed at nearby ancient burial mounds, together with pots, tools and weapons dating back to as early as 10,000BC. The grounds are dominated by the bizarre and grandiose Peace Tower, which, curiously, was erected in 1940. At that time it had a different name: Hakko-ichi-wu ('Eight World Regions Under One Roof'), em-

The long beach at Miyazaki

bodying the militarist aims of the Imperial Japanese Army. More palatable in its goal is the park's Miyazaki Shrine, dedicated to Japan's quasi-legendary first emperor, Jimmu, who reputedly commenced his glorious career in this region.

Fiery Kyushu

Throughout history the leaders and people of Kyushu have been known for their independence and feistiness. The region's typically hot cuisine mirrors this.

Just north of Miyazaki is one of the many results of Japan's grandiose spending projects that characterised the 'bubble economy' years of the 1980s and early 1990s. **Seagaia Ocean Dome**, one of the world's largest indoor water parks, comprises an artificially landscaped beach complete with palm trees and a giant wave pool to complete the illusion of a tropical paradise. The facilities are enclosed within a huge retractable roof.

South of Miyazaki, **Aoshima**, a seaside resort with plenty of action and animation of the modern kind at its beaches, cafés, hotels and amusement arcades, is the most popular stop on the line. Patronised by sun-worshippers and weekend surfers, Aoshima's main drawcard is its tiny subtropical island of the same name, surrounded by great platforms of 'devil's washboard', eroded rock formations, row upon row of shallow pools and indented octopus-shaped rings sunk into long furrows of basalt which disappear at high tide.

Beyond Aoshima the picturesque, winding Nichinan coast alternates rugged cliffs with some fine sandy bathing beaches. The seafood along this coast is especially good: try the reasonably priced lobster and giant periwinkles. Visitors can continue south for another few stops on the delightful, two-carriage Nichinan line train to the old samurai town of **Obi**. Only a discerning few Japanese visitors file in and out of Obi's gardens and samurai villas, a measure of how little visited this town of time-worn shrines, temples, oak, cedar and cryptomeria trees, is. At the core of the old quarter, 15 minutes on foot from Obi Station, less on one of the bicycles that can be hired from the station kiosk, Otemon-dori, a ramrod straight avenue lined with old houses, plaster storerooms and stone and clay walls topped with ceramic tiles, leads to the superbly restored Otemon, or main gate, the entrance to the carefully restored castle grounds.

Southern Kyushu

Kagoshima dominates the head of a deep indentation at the southern tip of Kyushu, and its harbour has played a prominent role in Japanese military history. It was here that the Portuguese landed,

The Okinawa Islands

Returned to Japanese sovereignty in 1972, after 27 years of postwar US occupation, Japan's own tropical paradise can be reached by plane (1 hour 35 minutes) from Fukuoka on Kyushu. The main attraction in this string of islands is island-hopping in search of perfect beaches and coral reefs, with some of the best swimming at Nakadomari's Moon Beach. Okinawa comprises 57 islands altogether, 40 of which are inhabited.

The main city on Okinawa's main island is Naha, which is overwhelmingly influenced by the postwar American military presence. The island's military bases are still home to tens of thousands of US servicemen and dependents. The vast selection of army surplus junk (such as bullet and shell casings) on sale in central Naha is certainly a strange one. Not surprisingly, there is a boisterous nightlife and busy red-light district – Naha was the friendly setting of the Marlon Brando film *Teahouse of the August Moon*.

Among Okinawa's many special attractions are the rural bullfights in the villages north of Naha. These contests pitch bull against bull on the same principle as sumo wrestling, as one entrant attempts to push the other out of the ring, not to kill him. The local taste in entertainment also runs to more grisly events: the public fights to the death between mongoose and cobra, staged by gamblers for high stakes.

Undeniably spectacular is Gyokusendo Cave, situated 12km (7½ miles) southwest of Naha, near the village of Minatogawa. Extending over 1.5km (1 mile), it is adorned by half a million stalactites and stalagmites among crystal-clear streams and hordes of friendly little bats.

bringing to Japan for the first time bread, guns and Christianity. The sailors' first landing was on the little offshore island of Tanegashima, which has progressed from matchlocks and muskets to being Japan's main rocket-launching centre.

It was from Kagoshima that the last desperate sorties of World War II were begun in order to resist an imminent US invasion, including the *kamikaze* raids on American warships. Inevitably, devastating bombing reprisals flattened the city. But modern Kagoshi-

In Shiroyama Park

ma is now an attractive green and airy place, with wide boulevards, delightful parks and a couple of intriguing historical museums. Kagoshima's smart new station now links the city with Tokyo by bullet train.

Shiroyama Park (southwest of Kagoshima Station) is up on a hill, giving you a fine view of the city and Kagoshima Bay through the archway of Nanshu Shrine. This shrine is dedicated to Kyushu's most celebrated son and one of Japan's national heroes, Takamori Saigo, last great champion of the samurai. He is buried with 2,023 of his warriors, who died in the ill-fated 1877 Satsuma Rebellion. This was the last stand of the samurai against the overthrow of their time-honoured privileges. Many of the soldiers, like Takamori himself, died by their own hand in a final gesture of defiance. A museum in the park (daily 9am–5pm), is devoted to his life and battles. The history of the Kagoshima region is nicely summed up in the ultramodern **Reimeikan Prefectural Museum** (Tue–Sun 9am–5pm), which includes local arts and crafts as well as examples of those first Portuguese matchlock rifles.

Sakurajima has erupted thousands of times since the 1950s

A few kilometres or so north of Kagoshima Station are the lovely **Iso Gardens**, also landscaped on a hill, where the lord of Satsuma had his villa. Be sure to visit the **Shoko Shuseikan Museum** (daily 8.30am–5.30pm), housed in an old factory established here by the forward-looking leader for arms manufacture and other new industries.

Out in the bay – towering over the entire peninsula – is Japan's most notoriously active volcano, the huge three-coned **Sakurajima**, which sends up tremendous black and white clouds of ash and steam. The mountain, which rises to 1,120m (3,670ft), has erupted more than 5,000 times since 1955, sending clouds of ash and often large boulders raining down on Kagoshima. (Umbrellas are used as much for ash as for rain.) Take a taxi or bus from Kagoshima Station for a closer look at the lava and a fine view of the whole Kagoshima Bay area. The Sakurajima peninsula was once an island until a gigantic eruption in 1914, when the rocks and lava joined it for ever to the mainland. A powerful illustration of the magnitude of the eruption is found at Haragosha Shrine, where you can just see the top cross bar of the shrine's arch; the rest submerged by hardened lava.

Local rulers welcomed Francis Xavier to Kagoshima, the first Japanese city he visited, in 1549. **St Francis Xavier Memorial Church**, in Xavier Park (tram to Takamibaba stop), was built in 1949 to commemorate the 400th anniversary of the arrival of the Jesuit missionary. His statue – inexplicably pinned halfway up a monolith in a very martyr-like pose, although he died in his bed (in China) – stands with its back to the sea beside a sculpted frieze dedicated to the suffering of his Japanese converts.

Ibusuki, to the south of Kagoshima, is a hot-spring resort that caters particularly for honeymoon couples – hundreds of them at a time. However, the main draw is its famous natural sand bath. Clad only in a cotton kimono, you lie down for attendants to bury you up to the neck in sand at a medium-broil temperature. Just stare up at the sky while you sweat off a few kilos and the attendant shovels on fresh sand. As the local chamber of commerce hilariously puts it: 'It is not only effective for overall beauty, but also for whiplash injuries caused by traffic accidents, and popular with newlyweds'. A more cynical view is that the sands provide a cure for which there is no known disease.

Chiran (80 minutes inland by bus from Kagoshima) is a peaceful, secluded 18th-century samurai village. In classically narrow, zigzagging lanes designed to hinder surprise attacks, the houses, today still inhabited by the Satsuma warriors' descendants, offer the rare opportunity to visit some exquisite private gardens, otherwise carefully concealed behind tall hedges. The

Buried alive: hot volcanic sand therapy at Ibusuki

特攻機 "零戦"
特攻隊の最高の遺品とて特攻機を展示

Kamikaze aeroplane, on display at Special Attack Peace Hall

simple, serene style of landscaping, with rocks, gravel and a few shrubs, draws on the precepts of Zen Buddhism that had such a special appeal for the austere samurai.

Be sure to try the local, volcanically enriched, purple sweet potato, which is also sold as ice cream. Chiran is surrounded by tea plantations. The local variety, *chiran-cha*, is considered one of the best green teas in Japan.

During World War II, Chiran served as a base for *kamikaze* raids on US shipping. The town's **Special Attack Peace Hall** (daily 9am–5pm), which includes a monumental statue of a pilot, exhibits the young men's uniforms, helmets and final letters to their families explaining that they were continuing the samurai spirit of defending the country's traditional values. There are also full-scale models of the planes, with a fuel tank big enough for only a one-way mission.

Western Kyushu

Halfway back along Kyushu's west coast, **Kumamoto** is an old castle town that was of considerable importance to the Tokugawa shoguns as a counterweight to the presence of the annoyingly independent Shimazu clan down in Kagoshima. For visitors today, Kumamoto serves as a convenient gateway for the scenic road trip to the Mt Aso volcano or a ferry cruise to the Unzen-Amakusa National Park.

The reconstructed **Kumamoto Castle** is worth a visit for the significant role it played during the last hectic days of Japan's feudal era. Once a vast fortification of 49 turrets, it ranked alongside Osaka and Nagoya as one of the country's greatest impregnable bastions. The 1960 ferroconcrete reconstruction of the main castle-keep houses a fine museum of feudal armour and weapons and offers a good view of the city. **Suizenji Park** is an extravagant but attractive example of the extensive gardens of the 17th century. Here, designers have reproduced a miniature version of all the major landscape features along the old Tokaido Highway between Kyoto and Edo – including, of course, a small artificial version of Mt Fuji.

The bus ride from Kumamoto to the mighty **Mt Aso** volcano takes you across some gently rolling hills, past orange groves, fields of watermelon and the special grass used for *tatami* mats. There is even a rare sight of yellow wheat fields – grown for beer and noodles rather than for bread (which is mostly imported). The panorama of the five volcanic craters of Mt Aso blends vivid emerald-green mounds with great carpets of pink azaleas on the

Paper carp streamers to celebrate Boys' Day

surrounding slopes and plateau. Only one of the craters, Naka-dake, is still really active. But it is well worth a visit to the top (a short hike from the bus stop) to peer down into the bleak, barren crater emitting puffs of sulphurous fumes and contrasting starkly with the colourful vegetation all around it.

On your way back down, allow enough time to visit the fasci-nating **Aso Volcanic Museum** (daily 9am–5pm). This has some very realistic audio-visual re-enactments of eruptions and earth-quakes, with special stereo sound effects. Three-dimensional mod-els of exploding mountains and molten lava flows from all over the world are shown. You can press a button to see America's Mt St Helens blow its top, or you can relive the astonishing 1933 erup-tion of Mt Aso itself.

The **Unzen-Amakusa National Park**, consisting of a peninsu-la and islands west of Kumamoto, is most pleasantly reached on a picturesque one-hour ferry trip from the nearby port of Misumi to Shimabara. The harbour is dotted with the pine-covered islands

Fishing nets on the quay, Unzen

of Tsukumo, offering delightful bathing along white-sand beaches. Unzen itself, once the favoured 'hill station' of Europeans escaping the steaming summers of the Asian mainland, is now a rather noisy, crowded spa resort. It serves best as an overnight stay prior to an early morning hike around the Unzen volcano's craters. The volcano last erupted in the spring of 1991, causing considerable death and damage, but it is no longer considered dangerous.

Nagasaki

Nagasaki is an unexpectedly charming city. To a large extent, this reflects its unbroken experience of more than four centuries of hospitality to foreigners – Chinese, Portuguese and Dutch – during a period in Japanese history when the country was characterised by

A cruel irony

Like Hiroshima, the name Nagasaki is immediately associated with the Atom bomb. It is a cruel irony that this weapon exploded in the town in Japan that was most famously open towards foreigners.

often murderous xenophobia. Its natural harbour, surrounded by green hills, is one of the most attractive in the world. Indeed, the city's distinct geography allowed most of its older neighbourhoods to survive the terrible destruction wrought by the second atomic bomb to be dropped on Japan, on 9 August 1945 – despite the fact that the Nagasaki bomb was more powerful than the one dropped on Hiroshima three days earlier.

Long before the arrival of the first Europeans, Nagasaki had been a major focus of Japan's trade with China. Indeed, the Chinese influence in the city is clearly noticeable even today. Major Buddhist temples, profiting from the suppression of Christianity during the 17th century, were established by Chinese Zen monks and designed in the style of the late Ming Dynasty.

On a more mundane contemporary level, the most popular Nagasaki lunchtime meal is a solid, nourishing bowl of *chanpon*: Chinese noodles in a tangy fish broth laden with a cornucopia of mushrooms, fish, prawns, vegetables and other goodies.

Near the centrally located Japan Railways station is the first sign of the Portuguese role in the city's fascinating history. A monument to 26 Christian martyrs executed in 1597 (at the beginning of Japan's repression of Catholicism) includes a small museum displaying relics, including a communion wafer that has survived in dehydrated form since the 17th century. The museum describes how other Christians were boiled alive in 1615 at the nearby Unzen hot springs. (Bear in mind, of course, that equally cruel religious persecution of Catholics, Protestants and Jews was quite common in Europe at that time.)

Even after the persecution and banishing of missionaries and the ban on Christianity, Nagasaki's Catholics still managed – at great risk – to continue clandestine observance throughout the years of the Tokugawa shogunate. They even went to Buddhist temples to worship the feminine Kannon deities, which were resculpted holding a child to represent Mary and Jesus.

The Dutch, however, being nonproselytising Protestants, were allowed to stay on throughout Japan's centuries of isolation. Their little community on Dejima Island, in Nagasaki Bay, sheltered the only remaining foreigners left in the country. *Oranda-san* ('Dutch people') eventually became the accepted term for all foreigners in Japan.

To get a good sense of Nagasaki's personality, start down at the harbour. Boat tours begin from the pier at Ohata Port Terminal, taking you on a fascinating 50-minute cruise around Nagasaki Bay. Your excursion steamer will feel like a child's toy as it passes the gigantic supertankers of the Mitsubishi Shipyard. Now the largest private shipyard in the world, this was the intended target that the US Air Force B-52 missed when it dropped the second atomic bomb. **Dejima Pier** has been reconnected to the mainland from what was once the Dutch island concession. The museum here, **Deji-**

Deadly delicacy

Although *fugu*, the pufferfish or blowfish, contains a potentially deadly toxin, it is a local speciality – one that is particularly tasty in winter. But it must be prepared properly; if it's not, the toxins can poison the eater.

Nagasaki's old town evaded destruction by the Atom bomb

ma Museum of History (daily 9am–5pm), has interesting relics of the Dutch community. In front of the museum is a model of the neat little settlement they established in 1609, when the only Japanese permitted to visit were trading partners and prostitutes. Commerce has always been an effective bridge of cultural barriers.

To see how the Dutch of a later era lived, climb the cobbled street of **Hollander Slope** (tram No. 5 to the Ishibashi stop), where you'll see some red-brick and wooden clapboard houses with colonial-style verandahs and – a rare sight atop houses in Japan – chimneys. The houses are an enduring monument to the privileged position of the foreigners allowed to live here.

The British presence in 19th-century Nagasaki is nostalgically commemorated at the hillside **Glover Gardens** – named after Thomas Glover, a prominent 19th-century trader – a short distance west of Hollander Slope. Escalators take you up to the houses of British traders, elegant mixtures of Japanese and European architecture. To the delighted curiosity of Japanese visitors, the houses are filled with Victorian paraphernalia: damask-covered furniture, an upright piano, a massive mahogany sideboard and a grand old gramophone with a big horn, manufactured by the Nippon-Ophone Company.

Kofukuji temple was the first of the Zen Buddhist temples built by the Chinese (1620) after the Tokugawa shoguns had outlawed Christianity and ordered citizens to register as Buddhists. In a picturesque setting with palm trees in the courtyard, the temple's architecture and sculpture are typical of southern China. Kofukuji also offers (by advance reservation) a frugal but tasty vegetarian meal cooked by the priests themselves. Meal times are announced by the beating of a big red 'fish' gong.

The pride and joy of the neighbourhood is the **Meganebashi**, a double-arched stone bridge across the Nakajima River. It was built in 1634 by the abbot of Kofukuji and is the oldest of its kind in the country. The reflection of the double arches in the river on a fairly calm day creates a visual image resembling a pair of glasses. The narrow streets bordering the river are full of interesting antiques shops, coffee shops and restaurants. **Sofukuji** temple (1629) is a handsome example of late Ming Dynasty architecture, with

What Kind of Army?

Article 9 of the postwar constitution, set up by the Americans, states that Japan is prohibited from possessing or having the potential of an external military force. In place of a military is the Jieitai, or Self-Defence Forces (SDF). Established in 1954, the SDF is a highly sophisticated military entity and one of the strongest armies in the world with nearly 300,000 troops, a situation that increasingly concerns Japan's neighbours. However, ships and planes in the SDF have limited operating range, and officially the SDF's responsibility extends 1,600km (1,000 miles) from Japan's shores.

With memories of Japan's aggression, Japan's military role today is a continuing and delicate debate, often igniting right-wing nationalists and conservatives. In 1992, a law authorised sending troops overseas in limited numbers and intended for non-combatant UN peace-keeping operations, such as in Cambodia.

its striking vermilion-painted, stone-arched tower gate. In the courtyard is a huge iron cauldron that was used for distributing rice gruel to the poor during famines in the 17th and 19th centuries. The Chinese Buddha statues here are notable for their variously proud, cheerful or humble stances not to be seen in the Buddhas of Japanese temples.

In the **Nagasaki Museum of History and Culture** (daily 8.30am–7pm), a few minutes' stroll east of the temple, local crafts, imported arts from continental Asia, painted screens depicting Dutch and British ships in the bay, and scale models reconstruct the history and development of the city.

Sofukuji, a magnificent Ming temple at Nagasaki

The **Nagasaki Peace Park** embraces the epicentre of the atomic blast that left 73,884 people dead, 74,904 injured and a miraculous 71,585 unscathed. The hills surrounding the city did much to contain the subsequent atomic fallout. The park features a monumental sculpture (by local artist Kitamura Seibo) that stirred considerable controversy when unveiled in 1955. The massive figure's right hand points skyward – towards the actual point of detonation – as a warning of the constant threat of nuclear weapons, while his left hand stretches out in a gesture of universal peace. As in Hiroshima, one of the most moving monuments is a single piece of masonry left standing. Here it is the red-brick and grey-stone remains of an arch from the Urakami Catholic Church, at the time the largest church in Asia.

Kitamura Seibo's huge statue in Nagasaki Peace Park

A visit to Nagasaki is meaningless without a stop at its **Atomic Bomb Museum** (daily, May–Aug 8.30am–6.30pm, Sept–Apr 8.30am–5.30pm), less elaborate than the one at Hiroshima, but provocative and challenging nonetheless. The exhibits powerfully document the build-up to the dropping of the atomic bomb on Nagasaki and the horrific effects of the blast itself and its aftermath. Simple objects – a melted bottle, the charred remains of a kimono – as well as photographs of victims provide stark evidence of the bomb's destructive powers. The curators have done a good job of separating any military justification for the decision from its tragic consequences for the civilian population. Like the Hiroshima museum, the final message is not of victims demanding sympathy but of an entire community committed to total nuclear disarmament for the sake of the entire planet, with its own message of 'Never again'.

Finally, a rewarding experience at the end of a long day is to take the cable car to the top of **Mt Inasa**, 332m (1,089ft) high, for a dramatic sunset view of Nagasaki and its harbour as the city lights begin to sparkle.

NORTHERN HONSHU AND HOKKAIDO

The regions of Japan to the northeast of Tokyo are more sparsely inhabited and less often visited by tourists, either foreign or Japanese. But both northern Honshu – which is more commonly known as 'Tohoku' – and the northernmost island of Hokkaido offer the advantage of unspoiled countryside and friendly down-to-earth villagers still imbued with something of a frontier spirit. Their folkcrafts are authentic and much less commercialised than in most other parts of Japan. And their festivals, in an area without the usual urban entertainment, are frequent, colourful and more spontaneous than in the more densely populated regions of the country. No picture of Japanese life is complete without a short visit to these northern territories.

Tohoku

Until the Tokugawa shoguns completed their conquest of all Japan from the 17th century on, the towns of **Tohoku** constituted the northern boundaries of the Japanese empire. Beyond them were the tribes of the native Ainu, at that time not considered 'Japanese'. It was only when the Ainu were progressively driven north up into Hokkaido that Tohoku was opened up to broader settlement.

The Poetry of Basho

Matsuo Basho, the pseudonym of Matsuo Munefusa (born 1644), is considered to be the greatest of Japan's *haiku* poets. Basho took the 17-syllable *haiku* form and enriched it with descriptive simplicity and contrast. Frequently used to describe Basho's poetry is *sabi* – the love of the old, faded, and unobtrusive.

A samurai for a local feudal lord, Basho moved to the Japanese capital city of Edo (now Tokyo) after his lord's death. In 1684, Basho made the first of many journeys through the islands, to Tohoku and written of in *Oku no Hosomichi (The Narrow Road to the Deep North)*, considered by many to be one of the most beautiful works in Japanese literature.

Its massive rice yield (over 20 percent of the national rice crop) has made Tohoku the chief supplier of the country's needs. Thus, the general trend for more and more peasants to drift away from the land to the cities has been less marked here. The very remoteness of Tohoku was appealing to such religious groups as the Zen Buddhists, who espouse an ascetic, unworldly life and constructed some of the country's finest Buddhist temples in this area.

Matsushima is considered one of the country's three Great Scenic Beauties (part of the Japanese passion for cataloguing things in three of this or eight of that). Although you can reach Matsushima in 40 minutes by train from Sendai, the best way is to stop off at Shiogama and take the one-hour boat cruise across Matsushima Bay. Scores of tiny islands dot the bay, their white sandstone shaped by the elements into arches, caves and pyramids and covered with lovely, wispy sea pines. The changing perspective as you cruise slowly past is extraordinary.

In the town of Matsushima, visit the pretty Kanrantei Pavilion for one of the best views of the bay from a rocky cliff beside the landing stage for the cruise ships. But practically any point on the hills rising behind the town will offer you a spectacular view. **Zuiganji** temple is the centre of an old Zen Buddhist seminary. The buildings were constructed in 1609 by the lord of Tohoku, Masamune Date. In the temple's treasure house you can see a statue of the crusty old warlord in all his armour. He lost his right eye – from smallpox, not in battle – and was nicknamed Dokugan-ryu ('One-Eyed Dragon'). As you walk up the long cedar-shaded avenue to the temple, notice the two-storey caves hewn from the rock that serve as accommodation for itinerant monks.

In the town of **Hiraizumi** – just a seven-minute train journey from Ichino-seki Station – you'll find a temple dating from the late Heian period (early 12th century). **Chusonji** was erected by the Fujiwara family when their power behind the imperial throne in Kyoto was waning. Two of the temple's structures have survived the countless wars of the Fujiwara. The Konjikido (Golden Hall)

The Matsushima coast is peppered with tiny islands

is a fabulously opulent mausoleum that Kiyohira Fujiwara built for himself in 1124. Everything except the uppermost roof covering is coated in pure gold. This priceless treasure, now protected by glass inside a fireproof concrete Kamakura-style hall, is believed to be what Columbus was after in his search for the country he called Chipangu. The Kyozo is even older (1108) and used to house the temple's Buddhist scriptures *(sutras)*, which are now kept in the modern treasure house. Hiraizumi showcases Japan's most intact Heian period garden, Motsu-ji temple's **Jodo-teien**. Little remains of the temple itself, founded by the Fujiwara in 850, but its paradise garden, lake, miniature islands and soft lawn are well preserved. Flowers bloom throughout the year; some 30,000 irises every June make an impressive sight.

A fruitful side trip from here, **Kakunodate** is a delightful feudal town with virtually intact samurai quarters. A few old samurai villas and gardens are open to the public. Pieces of *kaba-zaiku*, a local craft involving the surfacing of boxes, tea caddies and furniture with cherry bark, are sold as the town's signature souvenir.

The bright lights of Sapporo

Hokkaido

Not opened up to full-scale settlement until after the Meiji Restoration of 1868, the island of **Hokkaido** is Japan's 'Far North'. Here are some of the few Japanese who enjoy uncrowded cities, unspoiled wilderness and a simpler existence in a climate and landscape comparable to Scandinavia: snowcapped mountains and pine forest, with a subarctic climate in the northernmost area. The island's capital, **Sapporo**, was a natural choice for Japan's first Winter Olympic Games in 1972. Yet in the summer months Hokkaido's mountains and lake country are mild enough for good camping and hiking. At the end of the 19th century unemployed samurai took their families to Hokkaido to carve out a new life for themselves. American advisers helped to develop Hokkaido's agriculture and coal-mining industries and to lay out an urban grid system for Sapporo.

In 2008, after years of neglect and discrimination, the government finally recognised the tiny but historically significant Ainu community as a distinct group, a triumph of sorts in a country that has always tried to cover up its ethnic diversity. Hokkaido now has some fascinating museums devoted to Ainu life, and the village of Shiraoi preserves the artefacts and folkcrafts of their culture.

Sapporo

One of the most attractive postwar urban innovations in Japan is Sapporo's **Odori Promenade**, a broad green boulevard lined with flower beds, lilacs and maples – and with fountains down the middle, running east to west for a straight mile. In the first week of February, this is the venue for Sapporo's world-famous Snow Festival. Snow statues and ice sculptures made by corporate, professional and amateur teams are decidedly complex and often quite large.

Sapporo has a nationwide reputation for its beer, introduced in the 1870s by a German brewer who recognised the surrounding country's hop-growing potential. The beer garden, to the northeast of the central area, is a lusty place to sample the town's frontier spirit.

Around the Island

Lake Shikotsu, a volcanic crater lake situated 26km (16 miles) west of Chitose airport, provides one of southern Hokkaido's most picturesque camping and hiking areas. There's great salmon fishing here each year starting in May. You won't find much Ainu culture left in Hokkaido, but not far from the spa town of Noboribetsu is **Shiraoi**, a reconstructed Ainu village with artisans demonstrating traditional arts and crafts. The superb **Ainu Museum**, established with the help of European and American anthropologists, features a vivid exhibition of Ainu history.

Hokkaido has many national parks. Untamed **Shiretoko National Park** in the island's far northeast is a Unesco World Heritage site, characterised by black rocks, virgin forests and abundant wildlife.

American influence

Farms on Hokkaido look similar to those in Iowa or Vermont thanks to the influence of American agricultural experts brought here in the early 20th century. Likewise, Hokkaido's urban streets have a broad American look and are spacious by Japanese standards.

WHAT TO DO

SHOPPING

Modern Japan has embraced the consumer society to such an extent that shopping can be a full-time pursuit. The Japanese themselves (in the big cities at least) can be seen more often than not with some kind of shopping bag – they make very large, sturdy ones – just on the off chance that they might want to buy something. You cannot get to know this country properly, even if you don't want to buy anything, without exploring the rich and varied range of traditional arts and crafts, the famous cornucopia of electronic gadgets and precision instruments, or the impressively awful selection of kitsch souvenirs in the major tourist centres.

The cost of living in Japan has not risen as much in recent years as in many other developed countries, but a stiff sales tax and surprisingly convoluted and inefficient distribution systems preclude very cheap buys. However, some bargains can still be had.

A good way to begin a shopping expedition is by looking at the range of goods in the department stores and hundreds of speciality shops in the underground shopping centres. Department stores generally offer superb selections of everything – but at Japan's highest prices. You can then go off to find better prices at discount shops.

You might be tempted to do your shopping at the end of your trip so you won't have to drag all that electronic equipment, lacquerware, ceramics, or whatever around the country with you. Instead, consider

Delicately painted traditional fans

Not such a bargain

Bear in mind that some Japanese consumer goods are available for far less overseas than they are in Japan. Japanese tourists visiting other countries are still shocked when they discover this.

Akihabara in Tokyo, known as 'Electric Town'

buying everything you want as you go along, using Japan's remarkably efficient and inexpensive *takkyubin* courier delivery services (available at the ubiquitous convenience stores) to forward your larger purchases to your hotel, where they will be waiting for you on your return to Tokyo or elsewhere. Given Japan's relatively low crime rates, you can be sure you'll be reunited with your precious souvenirs.

Hi-Tech Products

In Tokyo, the place to go for every electronic and computer item imaginable – and plenty that you didn't even know existed – is Akihabara, an entire district devoted to speciality shops selling mountains of electronic equipment often at low prices. The larger stores usually have a tax-free department offering a narrower range of products designed for use abroad. English-speaking sales staff are often on hand, but don't expect the same discount prices that are offered on the other floors, despite the tax-free incentive.

One draw for visiting gadget freaks is being able to buy the very latest equipment several months ahead of its sales launch abroad. However, cameras and electronic goods are rarely available at better prices than those in New York City, still the world's reigning discount centre. Those hunting for computer software and hardware may have difficulties finding non-Japanese-language products for sale.

Osaka's equivalent hi-tech shopping district is Nipponbashi, but it does nothave the range or prices available in Akihabara.

Note that local electric current is 100 volts/50 (or 60) cycles, which is slightly different from the US and completely different from Europe. Therefore, if you don't want to bother with converters, stick to the top-floor tax-free department specialising in export goods designed for use around the world. Also note that Japanese TVs are designed for NTSC, the same broadcast system used in North America. If you plan to buy anything for use in Europe or elsewhere (where PAL is the main broadcast standard), make sure you purchase a multi-system unit; only these are compatible with the various broadcast standards in use around the globe.

Cameras. As an exception to the rule of not making big purchases until near the end of your visit, it makes sense to buy camera equipment as soon as possible so you can try it out during the trip. If a fault occurs, you can arrange to have it repaired or exchanged before you leave. Most stores are good about exchanging faulty goods. Note that warranties are often valid in Japan only, so check with the maker for details of upgrading to worldwide coverage. Shinjuku and the Ginza have Tokyo's largest discount camera stores.

Traditional Goods

Kimono. Japanese silk kimono are magnificent but staggeringly expensive. Most Japanese people save up for years to buy one and then often spend an equal amount of time in debt after making the investment. If you're not among the world's wealthiest tourists, the good news is that new and nearly new kimono are usually sold for a tiny fraction of their new prices at the big flea markets

Real silk kimono

Fine-quality parasol

held at temples, shrines and other large communal sites. In Tokyo, try the flea market (first and fourth Sundays) at the Togo-jinga, a shrine just a few steps from Harajuku's fashion street, Takeshita-dori. Kyoto's two biggest flea markets are held at Toji temple (the 21st of each month) and at Kitano Temmangu shrine (25th), but there are many others. Another alternative is the more modest but still elegant *yukata* (light cotton kimono), traditionally in indigo-blue and white and much cheaper than anything made of silk. Also look out for the silk *obi* sashes used to tie kimono. Some are magnificently decorative in their own right; if you don't want to wear one, consider an *obi* as an original and unusual wall-hanging in a Western home.

Antiques. Kyoto's famous geisha district of Gion has one of the finest selections of antique furniture and other items in Japan. Even if you're just browsing, the shops on Nawate-dori, Furomonzen-dori and Shinmonzen-dori offer a superb selection of antique furniture, ceramics, masks, lacquerware and Buddhist objects.

Artwork. Attractively colourful *ukiyo-e* woodblock prints and scroll paintings can be found in antiques shops, second-hand bookshops and even temple markets. Prices vary enormously.

Pottery and ceramics. These are very much a living tradition that has maintained its high standards. Most regions have their own distinct styles, varying from Kyoto's ornate and highly glazed *kiyomizu-yaki* to the beautiful natural earthenware of Bizen in Okayama and of Shigaraki near Kyoto. The town of Mashiko, north of Tokyo, is well worth a day's train excursion if you are interested in seeing how some of Japan's most celebrated pottery is made; the prices here are slightly better than back in Tokyo. You can also stay for lessons.

Lacquerware. You are least likely to go wrong in terms of uniformly high quality if you're in the market for lacquerware. Trays, plates, bowls and jewellery boxes are superbly finished – and not so heavy as to create problems of excess baggage.

Paper goods. Fans, dolls and hand-made stationery are usually reasonably priced but produced with the same meticulous care as are objects made from more precious materials.

Books. Tokyo's Kanda district is devoted almost entirely to second-hand books. The biggest neighbourhood of its kind in the world, it sells books in most European languages as well as Japanese. You'll also find excellent old maps and prints here, but the merchants know the going price for everything; real bargains are few and far between. Japanese **manga** comic books, a big export now, can be found almost anywhere.

In Tokyo, Shibuya and Shinjuku are the places to go.

Exquisitely made paper fans

ENTERTAINMENT

For information on all current Tokyo theatre programmes and show times, consult the free weekly magazine *Metropolis*, which is available in your hotel and in the foreign book sections of the Kinokuniya and Maruzen bookshops. The monthly magazine *JSelect* and the quarterly *Tokyo Journal* also carry listings of events.

As one of the most vivid and important expressions of Japan's traditional cultural heritage, theatre is an adventure in itself. Traditional Japanese drama, because of its stylisation, extravagant gesture and solemn or even bizarre intonation, might be difficult for Westerners to understand. However, perseverance will be rewarded once you get used to the conventions. The impact of the impassioned performances, aided by stunning costumes and elaborate make-up and masks, can be seductive; many a sceptic has emerged an addict. Most Japanese theatre aims less at developing a coherent plot, in the Western manner, than at creating a particular tone, atmosphere and emotional extremes.

Noh

This is the oldest theatrical form, strictly speaking, and also the most austere and demanding. Derived originally from ritual dances of the imperial court at Nara and Kyoto, in the 14th century *noh* became a fully developed masked drama of chanting, dancing and highly stylised acting. A hero and just two or three supporting actors enact stories about gods, historic battles, ghosts, unhappy love and grief-stricken insanity. The more sombre themes alternate with *kyogen* farces about the life of the common people, which often feature a satirical element.

The commentary is chanted by a chorus of six to eight narrators (reminiscent of the chorus in Greek tragedy) who sit at the side of the stage, while musicians positioned at the back of the stage provide stark accompaniment with flute and drums. Contrasting with the resplendent costumes, the set has an austere simplicity: a backdrop (usually a permanent wall) of a large pine tree and some bamboo, with no curtain. The stage is framed by a classical Japanese tiled roof making a 'house' inside the theatre.

Male actors, in masks, play all the roles. Characters often take several minutes to enter and exit the stage, moving painfully slowly in one of Japan's greatest examples of form over function. For aficionados, a *noh* performance is an eclectic nirvana. For many others, it is powerfully soporific. Look around the audience and you'll see plenty of locals nodding off unselfconsciously.

Noh, an age-old form of masked drama

Performances last several hours, with as many as five plays in a programme. You can probably manage at least a couple, and theatres often provide a good buffet between plays. See the best ones at Tokyo's National Noh Theatre, Kanze Kaikan at Shibuya, or Kyoto's National Noh Theatre. Other fine troupes perform in Osaka and Kanazawa.

Kabuki

Ever since the Tokugawa shoguns restricted performances to the samurai classes, *noh* drama has had a rather élitist appeal. *Kabuki*, on the other hand, has proved much more popular. Equally stylised in its way, *kabuki* is filled with fantastic colour, movement, action, drama and comedy. The performers are folk heroes, and the greatest of them – descendants of centuries-old dynasties of actors – are declared 'Living National Treasures'. Audience participation is at fever pitch, with people yelling as their personal heroes enter: 'We've waited for you!' or 'You're the greatest in Japan!'

Nothing is spared in the way of costumes and décor; there is no such thing as 'over the top'. Ever since the 18th century, revolving stages and trapdoors have been employed for supernatural characters to rise to the stage. Popular, but art of the highest order, *kabuki* tells stories of horror, blood and thunder, and passionate love. Connoisseurs wait for the set pieces: the colourful parade of the courtesan, a poignant s*eppuku* suicide, the exciting fight scenes and – summit of the art of *kabuki* – the end of a love affair that the heroine must break off, perhaps to save her lover's honour, but never because she no longer loves him.

'She' is in fact likely to be a 60-year-old man. In the early days of *kabuki,* at the beginning of the 17th century, the acclaimed Kyoto dancers started to present increasingly erotic and lascivious performances. With the audience's passionate loyalties to various star performers often leading to fights, the prudish Tokugawa shogunate decided to ban female performers, fearing a breakdown in the all-important social order. However, they then found that the young men who took over the female roles were also attracting ardent devotees among military officers and even priests – homosexuality at that time was not frowned upon. So they were in turn replaced by older men. After years of study, these *onnagata* make an astoundingly subtle and delicate art of capturing the gestures and movements of both young girls and old crones.

At Tokyo's Kabuki-za Theatre, you can hire headphones for the performance, providing simultaneous English-language translation of the important dialogue along with explanations of the action and conventions. Shows last up to four hours, but you can buy cheaper balcony tickets for just part of the programme. Kyoto's *kabuki* troupe performs in December and Osaka's in May.

Bunraku

Japan's celebrated puppet theatre can be seen at the National Bunraku Theatre in Osaka's Nipponbashi district, although performances are also put on several weeks each year at Tokyo's National Theatre. Don't be misled: *bunraku* is theatre for adults rather than children, using the same dramatic themes, stories and conventions as in *noh* and *kabuki* but achieving a unique impact with the almost life-sized, colourfully costumed puppets.

The puppeteers, dressed all in black, are initially distractingly visible on stage, manipulating and walking around with their puppets – yet they completely 'disappear' from your perception as the magic of the drama sweeps you away. A detailed English explanation of the plot is always provided, and wireless recorded commentary units are sometimes available. *Bunraku*'s heyday was at the beginning of the 18th century, when playwright Monzaemon Chikamatsu wrote works specifically for the puppets that are regarded as among the greatest achievements of Japanese literature. Heroism in battle and the noble values of the samurai tradition are the principal themes. It comes as quite a shock to watch a warrior performing his final gesture of ritual suicide and realise that it's only a puppet. The emotional effect is undiminished, and the gory effects are horribly creative.

Dancer in traditional costume

Film

Economically speaking, Japan's cinemas are in a lingering recession with audiences opting to watch DVDs at home; but in the industry itself there is no lack of talented directors and actors. Although Hollywood movies dominate box office returns, European art films are immensely popular. So too are violent gangster dramas and nostalgic films set in the late '50s and '60s, when life was simpler and families and neighbours looked out for each other. Mercifully, serious Japanese films are still being made, with many directors winning prizes at international film festivals.

Nightlife

You'll find good quality jazz bars, nightclubs and even country-and-western saloons in Tokyo's cosmopolitan restaurant districts of Akasaka and Roppongi.

Japan has a vibrant live music scene with its own home-grown brand of music called J Pop. Top international acts, from the Beatles to Britney Spears, have clamoured to perform in Japan, the world's second largest music market. Besides concert halls and rock venues like the Tokyo Dome, domestic and foreign rock bands appear in clubs called live houses. Some of the best live houses are in Shinjuku, Shibuya and Shimokitazawa.

Anime

The fantastic cartoon world of Japanese *anime* has legions of fans worldwide. Born of *manga* (comic books read by young and old) these feature-film and television cartoons are a far cry from the animated fare that most Westerners are raised upon. Some are aimed at children but these are so visually frenetic they make Looney Tunes seem mellow by comparison. The more adult fare is marked by violence, sexuality and often apocalyptic views of the future. The best work includes Otomo Katsuhiro's 1989 classic *Akira*, Oshii Mamoru's *The Ghost in the Shell* and works by Miyazaki Hayao, dubbed the Walt Disney of Japan.

FESTIVALS AND FOLKLORE

Despite increasing urbanisation and social change, Japanese society retains its small, closely knit communities strongly dependent on Shinto gods to ensure good harvests for survival. Forget the karaoke, the bullet trains and all those mobile phones for a moment. With such a highly developed sense of ritual and tradition, Japan's *matsuri* (festivals) are much more than just fun for the community: for many they remain integral to life itself. There is at least one festival happening somewhere in Japan on any day of the year.

The entrance to Kabuki-cho, centre of Tokyo nightlife

Each region has its own festivals or variations on the large national ones. Most honour either Shinto deities and shrines or major Buddhist temples. Buddhist festivals are usually fairly restrained affairs, often involving an important image of the Buddha that might be available for public viewing only on this occasion. The real drama is at Shinto festivals. Some are austere purification ceremonies involving traditional music, chanting, dance and often fire. At the opposite extreme are massive, almost riotous processions of thousands of bellowing, sweat-drenched men fighting to carry a huge portable shrine through the streets to a symbolic destination. Such is their exuberance and rapture that real outbreaks of violence can occur. These events have to be seen to be believed: they demonstrate the perfect flip-side of the supposedly reserved Japanese character.

Festivals are where superficially modern Japan gives way to the old, where ancient traditions are upheld, especially in remote rural districts. But there is usually a strong commercial aspect to the celebrations. Some rural communities devise small but colourful festivals to galvanise community spirit and the local economy by attracting badly needed domestic tourists.

Many festivals, though, are so spectacular that it is worth planning your visit specifically so you can attend. Definitely check with your nearest Japan National Tourist Office (JNTO) for information when planning your trip. Note that since many festivals follow the lunar calendar, the actual dates vary from year to year. With thousands of festivals and ceremonies taking place annually, this entire book wouldn't provide enough space to describe them all. Instead, we offer a sampling of large and small festivals, month by month. But when planning a visit, some supplementary research will probably uncover unexpected nuggets.

January. In Japan, New Year's Day is the big festival, closest in spirit to Christmas in the West, the time when relatives and friends visit each other and local shrines. New Year's Eve is a more solemn affair than in the West, when the Japanese flock to shrines to pray for good fortune for the coming year. People decorate houses, shops, offices and even cars with bouquets of pine and bamboo, symbols of evergreen stability and upright behaviour. In Tokyo on 2 January, the inner grounds of the Imperial Palace are opened to the public, with thousands coming to pay their respects to the emperor and enjoy a closer peek at his palace than is possible during the rest of the year.

Playing a bamboo flute

Closet pyromaniacs should not miss Nara's Wakakusa-yama Yamayaki or Turf Burning ceremony on 15 January, when people dressed as warrior monks burn the entire hillside of Mt Wakakusa after sunset, creating one of the year's most photographed spectacles, visible from miles around. The 15th is also Coming-of-Age Day nationwide, a milestone event for 20-year-olds attaining the age of majority. They attend special ceremonies at local community halls, and women dress in unusually opulent fur-trimmed kimono worn only on this special day.

February. The important *setsubun* festival marks the end of winter around the country on 3–4 February. With demons represented by priests wearing

Young women aged 20, entering adulthood

fearsome masks, onlookers throw beans to drive them away while shouting, 'Demons out, good fortune in!' The 3rd is also one of the two occasions each year when the 3,000 lanterns of the Kasuga Grand Shrine in Nara are lit. (The event is repeated on 14–15 August.) Up in Hokkaido, Sapporo holds its internationally popular Snow Festival (during the first or second week of February). The highlight is an ice sculpture competition at Odori Park, with huge superbly detailed models of castles, towers and giant characters both traditional and modern. Throughout Japan, children living in snowy areas look forward each year to the Kamakura Festival, when they build igloo-type snow houses.

March. On 3 March is the Hina Doll Festival, a special event for young girls. Exquisitely detailed dolls in ancient costumes repre-

Lucky *Hina* dolls

senting the imperial couple and other aristocrats are displayed for good luck. Some shrines display thousands of dolls brought by the faithful. Another annual highlight is the two-week O-Mizu-tori Festival at Nara's Nigatsudo Temple, one of Todaiji's subtemples. Although the central event is a solemn and highly symbolic water-drawing ceremony, the crowds turn out in force for the more public and spectacular fire ceremonies. Every night from the 1st to the 14th, in a highly dramatic display clearly designed to entertain, temple priests brandishing long poles with a flaming cedar ball at each end run along the front of the verandah, deliberately showering the large crowd below with burning embers (believed to bring good luck for the coming year, having burned away the transgressions from the previous one).

Another visual treat in March is the annual fertility festival held at Tagata Jinja in Aichi Prefecture, north of Nagoya. This amazing shrine celebrates an object that transcends borders and cultural barriers: the human penis. Phalluses huge and humble, wooden and stone are enshrined and worshipped here. And on 15 March each year, the mightiest specimen, a 2m (6½ft) monster made of Japanese cypress and weighing over 270 kg (600lb) is slowly carried through this small town, bulging out of its portable shrine. See it and you still won't believe it.

April. On 8 April the Buddha's birthday is celebrated with flower festivals held throughout Japan. The best place to view the spring azaleas is at the Azalea Festival in the last week of April at Tokyo's Nezu shrine. In the Kansai region, peony lovers head for Hasedera Temple in rural Nara. April is also cherry blossom season, with blossom-viewing picnics *(hanami)* held in parks and temples throughout Japan as the cherry-blossom 'front' makes its steady progress northwards. On the 14th and 15th the city of Takayama in Gifu Prefecture holds one of Japan's greatest processions of large, colourful floats.

May. The end of April into early May is Golden Week, the unofficial name for the conjunction of three major national holidays (Green Day, Constitution Day and Children's Day). Since this is the only time many Japanese are permitted to take a holiday, it is the worst time to visit Japan, since every hotel, inn, train and even plane is booked up months in advance. Although Boys' Day was officially renamed Children's Day to include girls, the reality is taking some time to catch on. This festival features giant carp streamers flying from poles *(see page 167)*. The carp's ability to struggle upstream against a strong current is regarded as a fit model for boys. On 15 May Kyoto celebrates its Hollyhock Festival (Aoi Matsuri). This ancient ritual is meant to pave the way for a good harvest, with branches of hollyhock to stave off thunder and earthquakes. The hollyhock decorates a huge red oxcart, accompanied from the Imperial Gosho Palace by 300 Kyoto citizens dressed in Heian-period costumes.

June. From June onwards, *ukai* celebrates the ancient use of cormorant birds to catch *aiyu*, a popular river fish. The animal rights movement has yet to penetrate Japan in any significant way: the cormorants' throats are constricted so they can't swallow the fish they catch underwater, and their owners retrieve the catch when the hapless birds resurface. The various events held around Japan are usually highly ceremonial, with blazing torches illuminating the proceedings.

Dragon dance

On 18 March the Golden Dragon dance is held at Tokyo's Senso-ji Temple (in Asakusa). A ceremonial carriage bears geisha playing traditional musical instruments.

Hundreds of paper banners at Toshogu shrine, Nikko

July. Kyoto's Gion Festival (officially the festival takes place throughout the month, but the high point occurs on the 17th) is the most elaborate procession of the year, with its grandiose floats and glowing lanterns. Originally, the festival invoked the help of the gods against a plague in medieval Kyoto; highly commercialised imitations of it are now celebrated all over the country. On the 24th and 25th, Osaka holds its flamboyant and mammoth Tenjin Matsuri, starting from the Temmangu shrine. It has fireworks, flaming torches and gaily decorated floats on the central Okawa River.

August. At the height of the summer swelter in July and August is *O-bon*, a colourful and joyous national Buddhist festival honouring the spirits of deceased ancestors. People travel around the country to clean their family tombs and gravestones. At Nagasaki in mid-August, glowing lanterns decorate the graveyards, while other lanterns are put out to sea on model boats to take the departed souls back to the other world. Like Golden Week in April–May, this is a great time to avoid Japan unless you relish competing for every train seat and hotel bed with millions of others. Many of the country's expressways come to a virtual standstill. On the 14th and 15th of the month is the year's second lighting-up of the thousands of lanterns at Kasuga Grand Shrine in Nara.

October. Mid- to late October is chrysanthemum viewing time, when flower displays are dotted around the cities.

November. The 15th is Shichi-Go-San (Seven-Five-Three), a ceremony for 5-year-old boys and 3- and 7-year-old girls. Children dress in kimonos or Sunday best and are taken to visit shrines.

December. The 14th is Gishi Sai, a memorial service for the 47 Ronin who, on this day in 1703, avenged the death of their master and later committed ritual suicide. They are buried at the Sengaku-ji where the service is held. On the 31st at the stroke of midnight, every temple bell throughout the country begins to toll. The bells toll 108 times representing the 108 evil human passions.

For complete details of these and other major festivals held annually in Japan, check the JNTO website at www.jnto.go.jp.

SPORTS

When the Japanese decide to do something, they seem to take a 'total-immersion' route, buying the latest outfits and equipment so that they look like seasoned professionals before they take a single lesson. This provides insight into the important Japanese concept of *katachi* (form), the rough equivalent of 'It isn't what you do; it's the way that you do it'. It is quite common to see Japanese men of all ages standing on train platforms or outside a building practising their stroke with an imaginary golf club.

Participant Sports

Tennis. With land prices notoriously high, urban courts are crowded and expensive, so your best bet is at the seaside or hot-spring resorts. If necessary, get your hotel to help you make reservations.

Golf. Unsurprisingly, golf is prohibitively expensive. You will have to share the Japanese golfer's manic obsession to want to shell out green fees of well over £50 at top clubs during peak periods. The best way to enjoy a round of golf is as the guest of a Japanese friend or business associate.

Swimming. Beaches close to Tokyo and Osaka are crowded (except after 1 September, when summer for the Japanese has officially ended). So you are better off going south to Kyushu, around Shimabara and the more secluded of the Amakusa Islands (for snorkelling and scuba-diving, too) or to the spa resort of Ibusuki. Water sports enthusiasts go south to the beaches of Okinawa, the liveliest being Moon Beach at Nakadomari.

Fishing. One of the joys of fishing in Japan is taking the catch back to your Japanese-style inn and having the cook grill it for you or turn it into sushi or sashimi (depending on your degree of faith in the cleanliness of Japan's highly polluted rivers). Freshwater angling – for bass, carp or trout – is good anywhere in the lakes and streams, best of all in Hokkaido, where you stand a good chance of hooking a salmon. Sea bream and sea bass are the most frequent catch in coastal waters. Ask about licence restrictions at local tourist offices.

Skiing. Japan has a number of excellent skiing areas, which quickly get crowded in season. Winter sports are one of Hokkaido's main draws for domestic tourism, with popular ski resorts at Teine Olympia (outside Sapporo), Niseko and Kiroro. Others are Zao (in Tohoku) and a number of resorts in Joshin-etsu Kogen National Park in the Japan Alps, where there are now splendid facilities thanks to the 1998 Winter Olympic Games in Nagano.

Spectator Sports

Baseball. The game is at least as popular in Japan as it is in the US. It was introduced in the 19th century, together with railways, cameras and whisky. Today baseball is big business, with cheerleaders, balloons and variations on US Major League hype. The major professional teams are owned by the biggest publishing empires or department store chains, each combining their company name with the time-honoured American nicknames, the most famous being the Yomiuri Giants. Japanese commentators have happily adopted the American jargon of 'Strike one, ball two', 'home

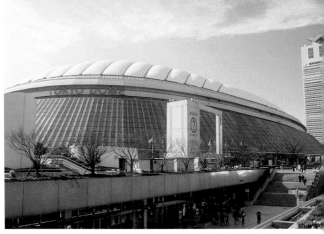

The Tokyo Dome

run' and 'pinch hit'. In Tokyo you can see games at the Tokyo Dome, and in Osaka at the Osaka Dome.

Sumo. Of the traditional Japanese sports, sumo wrestling is the most popular. This ancient sport originated more than 15 centuries ago in Shinto ceremonies. Today, sumo champions – the only men still allowed to wear the samurai warrior's gleaming top-knot hairdo – are national heroes and are much in demand for TV commercials. At the national level, there are a total of 575 wrestlers classed in six divisions according to their win-loss ratio in the annual tournaments. The highest division is the *makuuchi*, of which the champions are known as *yokozuna*. These giants weigh anything from 90 to 165kg (200 to 350lb), yet they have grace, dignity and suppleness that belie their massive bulk.

The *dohyo-iri* (ring entry) ceremony to open the tournament is a fascinating spectacle. The champions strut into the arena in richly embroidered silk 'aprons' covering the solid band protecting their midriffs. Salt is tossed across the *dohyo* (a raised mound of hard clay some 4.6m/15ft in diameter under a large suspended Shinto-roof-style canopy) to rid it of evil spirits. The sumo then swagger around and start the all-important 'psyching-out' of the opponent.

Pointedly avoiding each other's eyes, they raise a massive leg into the air (to a height that would do a professional dancer proud), slam it down with a mighty thud and lower themselves into the characteristic squat. This goes on for up to five minutes – all part of the great ritual build-up of tension before the wrestlers clash. Note that indulging in these highly stylised opening theatricals is a privilege of top-ranked wrestlers only.

The aim is for one wrestler to force the other out of the ring or to make him touch the floor with anything other than his feet. The bout is usually over in one or two minutes, sometimes mere seconds, but the intensity of the struggle and the sheer visual drama make for compelling entertainment.

Sumo wrestlers in action

Sumo tournaments are held in January, May and September at the Ryogoku Kokugikan in Tokyo, during March in Osaka, in July in Nagoya and in November in Fukuoka (Kyushu). The bouts commence in the morning, but the real crowds start arriving only in late afternoon. A little known secret is that a standing ticket (usually around £20) gives you the run of the arena: you can move around freely, sit in unoccupied seats and even enjoy the action from the ringside until the actual ticket-holders arrive later on. If you can, go out of your way to spend a few hours of watching live sumo. There is simply nothing on earth like it.

The Martial Arts

Most martial arts practised today came from China, Japan and Korea and share common techniques. There is no one superior style. Two major types evolved in Japan: the *bujutsu*, or ancient martial arts, and *budo*, or new martial ways. Both are based on spiritual concepts embodied in Zen Buddhism. *Bujutsu* emphasises combat and willingness to face death as a matter of honour. It contains the philosophy and techniques of the samurai warriors and includes *jujutsu* and *karate-jutsu*. *Budo*, started in the late 1800s, focuses on moral and aesthetic development. *Karate-do*, *judo* and *aikido* are all forms of *budo*. Most of the martial arts end in the suffix -*do*, usually translated as 'way' or 'path'. So, *kendo* is the way of the sword. *Do* is also the root of *dojo*, the place where one studies and practises a martial art.

Judo/jujutsu. The original form of *judo*, called *jujutsu*, was developed in the Edo Period (1603–1868). It was made up of different systems of fighting and defence, primarily without weapons, against either an armed or bare-handed opponent on the battlefield. The basic principle of the *judo* technique is to utilise the strength of the opponent to one's own advantage.

Karate. Meaning 'empty hand', *karate* is a form of unarmed combat in which a person kicks or strikes with the hands, elbows, knees or feet. It developed around the 1600s on the island of Okinawa. A Japanese clan had conquered the island and passed a strict law banning the ownership of weapons.

Aikido. This is a system of self-defence derived from the traditional weaponless fighting techniques of *jujutsu* and its use of immobilising holds and twisting throws, whereby an attacker's own momentum and strength are made to work against him.

Kendo. *Kendo* is Japanese fencing based on the techniques of the samurai two-handed sword. It is a relatively recent term that implies spiritual discipline as well as fencing technique.

Ninjutsu. Meaning 'the art of stealing in' or espionage, *ninjutsu* is practiced by *ninja*. Mountain mystics developed the art in the late 1200s, when *ninja* were masters at all forms of armed and unarmed combat, assassination and in the use of disguises, bombs and poisons. Although the rulers of Japan banned *ninjutsu* in the 1600s, the *ninja* practised it secretly, preserving its techniques. Today, it is a traditional martial art with a non-violent philosophy.

EATING OUT

If Japanese culture expresses itself most vividly in its food, that is also where the ultimate adventure for foreign visitors lies. The preparation and presentation of Japanese cuisine reflect the traditional emphasis on form, colour and texture. Any fine Japanese meal is supposed to be a feast for the eyes as well as the palate. The many small bowls and dishes in a typical meal, for instance, are chosen to suit the individual foods they contain.

The secret of enjoying Japanese food is to abandon all preconceptions about what a meal should be and how it should be served. Things you are used to eating hot will be served in Japan at room temperature, and dishes you expect to arrive separately will appear all together – or vice versa. Even people who consider themselves reasonably familiar with Japanese cuisine will find themselves baffled by much of what they encounter in Japan.

This island nation's huge dependence on fish and seafood is famous. Less well known is the fact that Japan has many indigenous vegetables, edible roots, grasses and even flowers that are simply not found elsewhere. As a result, many meals you are served will contain items that you have never seen before. Tackle these enthusiastically; you are unlikely to find much that is other than wholly delicious. After all, a standard Japanese meal is hardly something from another planet.

A typical traditional meal includes a main dish of cooked chicken, fish or meat, a few small vegetable dishes, pickles, *miso* (soybean paste) soup and the ever-present rice. Note that

Energy food

Some Japanese dishes are known as *stamina ryori*, dishes intended to raise energy levels. A popular dish is *unagi*, or broiled eel served on rice. It's said to help one withstand the hot and humid Japanese summer. Rich in vitamins E and A, it exceeds pork and beef in protein content, yet contains fewer calories.

Japanese gastronomy, a feast for the eyes and the taste buds

with a *teishoku* (set meal), you order only the main dish by name; the rest comes automatically, which makes things pretty straightforward. However, spare your server or host an interrogation as to the name and nature of every ingredient, many of which have no English equivalent.

Also, don't be offended or intimidated if people stare at you while you're eating. You – as the honourable visitor – are merely being observed for signs of approval. Give them a smile and an 'Oishii!' ('Delicious!') and you'll make their day.

Etiquette

Don't be daunted by the prospect of arcane rules of etiquette when confronted by your first Japanese dinner, whether formal or casual. The Japanese are taught that their food, like their language, is so impenetrable to outsiders that they consider even the most token effort heroic.

First, we offer a few simple tips. Taking off your shoes before stepping on a *tatami* mat should be obvious. But if you're not comfortable kneeling for long on the floor in the formal Japanese-style, just sit cross-legged like most of the population, especially men. Incidentally, that marvellous wet towel *(oshibori)* you receive to freshen up at the beginning of the meal should be neatly rolled up when you've finished with it. Don't, however, use it on anything except your hands.

Eating with chopsticks involves resting the inside stick firmly against the hand while moving the other like a pen to grasp your prey. However badly you cope, don't be surprised when your Japanese friends compliment you profusely – another admirable effort by their esteemed guest.

When drinking beer or sake (or anything else) with companions, you should serve your neighbour but not serve yourself, even if you have your own little jug in front of you. Your host will insist on doing the honours. Always hold your cup or glass when someone is pouring for you, to show your appreciation. For soup, take the small items of food using your chopsticks and drink the broth directly from the bowl, as there'll be no spoon. Make all the noise you like; it's not only expected but considered a compliment to the chef. Most Japanese slurp loudly when eating noodles, sucking them in with gusto. The extra intake of oxygen is said to improve the taste – but novice slurpers should beware of hyperventilating.

Japanese haute cuisine

Where to Eat

The high-class places *(ryotei)* serving Japanese haute cuisine live up to their international reputation for being eye-wateringly expensive. Given the meticulous preparation and the quality of the ingredients, the prices are perhaps justifiable. Generally, though, they are for the well-to-do and for businessmen on expense accounts. Nevertheless, you should consider budgeting for at least one elaborate Japanese dinner in a fine restaurant – many of which serve excellent food at more reasonable prices.

One economical way to do this is to stay at a traditional Japanese inn *(ryokan)*, where the price usually includes a superb dinner followed by an equally impressive breakfast the next morning. If you're lucky enough to have time to explore Japan beyond the confines of Tokyo, consider saving for a fine meal in one of the great gourmet centres such as Kyoto or Osaka or the major towns of Kyushu. There,

A street vendor's tasty snacks

you'll be sampling regional delicacies at their freshest while avoiding paying the premium of eating in Japan's most expensive city.

But more than most countries, Japan is blessed with excellent small, modestly priced restaurants serving typical Japanese food of very high quality. Many of these have a single speciality, as evidenced in the establishment's name: *sushi-ya*, *yakitori-ya* or *okonomiyaki-ya*. All have a short cloth curtain *(noren)* over the door; if it's fluttering outside, they are open. Even if you can't read the writing on the sign, many advertise their fare with a window display of astonishingly realistic plastic replicas of the food served within. These imitations of meat, fish, vegetables, rice and noodles are a great help in ordering your meal. If the menu has no explanation in English, just step outside again with the waiter and point to what you want.

If you don't want to restrict yourself to one particular cuisine, try an *izakaya*. Often called Japanese 'pubs,' these are really restaurants catering for enthusiastic drinkers rather than bars with food. *Izakaya* are lively, informal restaurants offering a bit of everything: sushi, *tempura*, *yakitori*, cooked fish, vegetables and salads, as well as strange interpretations of Western sundries such as chips and pizza. *Izakaya* are usually packed to overflowing on Friday nights, when the nation's increasingly pressured office workers go out with friends or colleagues.

Lowest on the social rung but no less worthy of your business are the street pushcarts *(yatai)* serving roasted sweet potatoes, noodles in soup *(ramen)*, stewed vegetables *(oden)* or grilled chicken. With a little roof to keep off the rain and stools for the customers, the vendors set up shop in entertainment districts such as Tokyo's

Plastic Fantastic

All visitors to Japan will soon notice the deliciously realistic models of meals featured in restaurant windows, designed to make choosing dishes easier. The manufacture of these plastic replicas is a whole industry in itself. It dates back to the Meiji Restoration of 1868, when the Japanese had to explain with models made of wax the new foods coming in from abroad.

Today's factories employ professional cooks to regulate the size, shape and colour of the 'food' to be made out of various vinyl resins. It has proved impossible for artisans other than real sushi cooks to compose convincing replicas of the little oblongs of raw fish on rice, but most ordinary craftsmen can manage a bowl of noodles all by themselves. Art students do the painting, and women assemble the finished product on its dish. The results are astonishingly realistic.

One of these 'meals' makes an unusual and humorous souvenir of your time in Japan; it will certainly last longer than the real thing. You can buy them from the factories' sales outlets, which are located in neighbourhoods specialising in restaurant equipment, such as Kappabashi in Tokyo and Doguyu-suji in Osaka's Namba. But these tasty titbits don't come cheap.

Kabuki-cho and Asakusa and Osaka's Shinsaibashi, or around major railway stations, doing their best business late at night.

Department store basements have become popular eating places, especially among trendy but thrifty office ladies. The food halls, called *depachika*, offer varied, well-balanced set lunches and self-service *bento*.

Kissaten are little coffee shops found everywhere. Before 11am, the price of a cup of coffee usually gets you a simple breakfast

Octopus is a popular ingredient in traditional Japanese cooking

(*mohningu saabisu*) with a slice of toast, hard-boiled egg and sometimes a mini salad. They also serve sandwiches, cakes and snacks.

Japanese 'take-away' food includes a sophisticated version of the packed lunch: the neat little box (*bento*) containing rice with fish or meat and various elegantly presented vegetable concoctions. In fact, so important is the *bento* in daily life that generations of mothers have traditionally competed to outdo each other with the boxes they prepare for their children and husbands.

What to Eat

With only a few exceptions, cooked food is usually served warm rather than hot. The Japanese don't feel it loses its flavour if you let it get cold while sampling something else, since many dishes are served simultaneously. Japanese rice is short grain and specially bred to be sticky (quite different from the 'dry' long-grain rice favoured in the West).

Breakfast

Although you might not welcome a Japanese-style breakfast every morning, do try it at least once. Not only is it low-fat, healthy and delicious, but it sustains you remarkably well for another day of arduous sightseeing. Since a traditional breakfast is not generally available in restaurants and coffee shops, Japanese inns are your best bet. The full version is likely to include grilled salted fish served at room temperature, hot *miso* soup with a few vegetables and *tofu* (high-protein white beancurd), a bowl of rice and tea.

Lunch and Dinner

One of the most popular Japanese lunches is *soba* (brown buckwheat noodles) served in a fish-based broth with a wide variety of added extras including fried beancurd, leeks, mushrooms, fish, chicken and other vegetables. One bowl makes a fine meal in the middle of a busy day. The thicker white noodles are called *udon* and the yellow curly Chinese ones *shinasoba*. Noodles may also be served cold (*zaru-soba* or *zaru-udon*), accompanied by a tasty soy-based dipping sauce to which you add fresh chopped onions, ginger and fiery *wasabi* (Japanese horseradish).

Chicken kebabs, known as *yakitori* – a tasty light meal

Udon is also served in a stew (*nabe*) containing fish, meat or chicken with vegetables and *tofu*, usually served in a cast-iron or heavy ceramic pot. A *nabe* is an informal traditional winter dish that is often shared by a group of people.

Another popular lunch staple is the *donburi*: a bowl of rice topped with a savoury mixture of cooked egg, onion, soy sauce and a main ingredient, usually a breaded pork cutlet (*tonkat-su*, another national institution), chicken or vegetables.

Gourmet on the go

Japan is a nation of obsessive train travellers, and some of its most popular foodstuffs are those sold at stations. A special type of *bento* that has become an art in itself, not to mention a pursuit for the connoisseur, is the *ekiben* (from *eki* for train station and *bento*). Trains often stop just long enough for passengers get off and buy their *ekiben*.

Donburi and noodle dishes occupy most of the window space in restaurants around the country serving lunches and light meals, so it's a good idea to get acquainted with them at an early stage.

Another keyword with which to arm yourself for lunch is the *teishoku*, which simply means 'set meal' (although 'setto' will get you understood in most restaurants). The main dish you order comes with vegetables, rice soup and pickles, a format which provides the best value meals in Japan. Restaurants located in the busy commercial centres of cities compete fiercely to attract office workers at lunchtime, and amazing bargains can be found as long as you can get a seat. (Try after 1pm to avoid the crowds.)

Taste and visual pleasure converge in sushi and sashimi, both prepared with uncooked seafood. *Sashimi*, usually served as a choice item within a larger meal, is premium raw fish sliced in bite-size pieces. It's dipped in a sauce you prepare to your own degree of spiciness from *wasabi* (mustard-like green horseradish – a little goes a long way), *shisonomi* herb-buds and soy sauce. The most common fish is tuna: *maguro* is the deep-red meat and *toro* the richer pink parts. Others are *tai* (sea bream), *sake* (salmon, but pronounced 'sha-keh'), *hamachi* (mackerel) and *aji* (pompano).

Sushi comes in two main types: *nigiri-zushi* is raw fish and (usually) boiled seafood on top of a patty of cold rice cooked with a little diluted vinegar to hold it together in an oblong shape. *Maki-zushi* are seaweed rolls, skinny or fat, filled with any combination of raw fish, seafood, vegetables and pickles.

The seafood used reflects the astonishing bounty of the teeming waters surrounding Japan: octopus, squid, clams, scallops, prawns and shrimps. When eating, try to turn the sushi upside down in the soy sauce so that only the fish is dipped; otherwise, the rice disintegrates – a

Fish is a mainstay of the Japanese diet

classic novice error. In sushi bars, you sit at a table with a selection of assorted fish and seafood. If you're not sure what specifically to order, ask for a selection; several combinations are always available at different prices.

Much more fun, though, is to sit where the real action is: up at the counter. Here you can choose the ingredients you want to try just by pointing (with a quick 'Sumimasen!' for 'Excuse me!'), then watch the sushi chef's dexterity as he deftly slices to create just the right shape (the result of years of training). Wash down your sushi with beer, cold or hot sake, or hot tea.

Sukiyaki (pronounced 'ski-yaki') was introduced only in the 19th century after the arrival of Americans demanding beef. Beginning as a characteristically inspired attempt to imitate – and ultimately surpass – the sailors' beef stew, the thin slices of tender beef are sautéed before you over a gas or charcoal fire. The meat is then stirred with translucent vermicelli, finely shredded green onions, mushrooms and greens (spinach or other green leaves). All the ingredients are appetisingly set out on a board beforehand. Tastiest by far is the fabled beef from Kobe: to give it flavour and keep it tender, the cattle are fed beer and lovingly massaged before being turned into beef.

For a do-it-yourself meal, try *shabu-shabu*, thinly sliced beef, which you boil in a pot set in front of you with chicken stock, cabbage, carrots, spinach, mushrooms and *tofu*.

Okonomiyaki is a very cheap do-it-yourself meal, especially popular with students and other young people. It's a Japanese-style savoury pancake containing chopped cabbage in an egg-based batter to which you add shrimp, squid, meat, or other ingredients. The whole thing is then prepared on the hot griddle built into your table. Someone is always on hand to show you how. As well as being great fun, an *okonomiyaki* or two can make a tasty lunch or dinner.

A warming winter favourite, *oden* is an informal hearty selection of stewed items more often sold by street vendors than by restaurants. You'll find everything stewing in the kelp-and-fish based broth: squid, seaweed, Japanese radish, potatoes, hard-boiled eggs, *tofu* and various meaty morsels.

Yakitori are wooden skewers with pieces of chicken barbecued and served with a savoury sauce. Various combinations of chicken parts, green onions, mushrooms and other vegetables are usually on the menu. *Yakitori* makes a great informal light dinner, usually with plenty of beer to wash it down.

Grilling squid

These lively, informal restaurants almost always feature a distinctive row of small red lanterns outside.

Tempura is a famous example of the Japanese transforming a foreign import into a unique and wholly original creation – in this case, Portuguese fritters prepared by the missionaries (the name probably comes from *têmpero*, the Portuguese word for seasoning). A typical selection includes a prawn or two, a mushroom, a small green pepper and slices of other vegetables, all coated in a light batter of egg and flour, deep fried and decoratively served along with a dipping sauce to which you then add grated radish and ginger.

If you have the chance, try *robatayaki*, which is simply anything you choose grilled in front of you on a large *robata* grill: fish, meat, seafood and numerous vegetables. Pointing at whatever you want transcends the language barrier. *Robatayaki* restaurants tend to have traditional rural décor and are usually atmospheric venues.

One of the world's supreme snack foods is the *onigiri*, a brilliant invention comprising a small triangle (or ball) of rice con-

Stall selling sweet and savoury biscuits made with rice flour

taining a filling of shredded salted salmon, seaweed, fish roe, or any of countless other ingredients, all enclosed in a wrapping of *nori* (seaweed). These are sold in the convenience stores which seem to adorn every main street; one or two are ideal for restoring the energy of fading tourists. Note the ingenious packaging separating the dry *nori* from the rice ball inside.

Japanese pickles

A meal always comes with *tsukemono*, or Japanese-style pickles. Ingredients include Chinese cabbage, bamboo, turnips, *kyuri* (cucumbers), hackberry, daikon, ginger and *nasu* (Japanese aubergine).

Despite the unfamiliarity of much of what you encounter, Japan has very few dishes that will shock a typical Western palate. For example, the Japanese (unlike many other Asians) are very conservative when it comes to meat, chicken and fish, discarding all but the choicest morsels. Don't worry about not knowing what something is; just dig in and enjoy!

Desserts

Traditional Japanese meals do not end with a dessert course. However, the Japanese definitely have a sweet tooth, as any visit to a coffee shop or department store will confirm. There you will find an amazing variety of Western-style cakes, pastries, fancy cookies and biscuits.

More interesting, though, is the seemingly infinite range of indigenous confections. Many of these are based on sticky rice and sweet red bean paste (with lots of added sugar) and fall somewhere between the categories of sweets and cakes. *Wagashi* is made from wheat or rice flour, mashed red beans, yams, arrowroot, egg and sugar. The moist sweets are known as *yokan*, a bean-paste jelly served in long rectangles and sliced. *Manju* are very popular sweet rice dumplings filled with red bean paste. All of these are very commonly given as gifts to friends and associates, as the exquisite department store displays (and prices) imply.

Savoury snacks are also very popular, especially *senbei*, the famous Japanese rice crackers that come in all shapes, sizes and flavours.

The Japanese hated milk when the Americans first suggested getting it from a cow, and ice cream has never caught up with Western standards. There is one interesting innovation in this domain: *matcha-aisu-kurii-mu*, or ice cream flavoured with green tea.

What to Drink

Whisky is considered the sophisticated alcoholic drink by middle-class upwardly mobile Japanese, although sake remains the national alcoholic beverage par excellence. Sake ranges from seriously rough stuff sold in machines to splendidly subtle creations prized by connoisseurs around the country. A colourless wine fermented from rice, it is drunk from thimble-sized cups. Heating actually destroys many of the subtle, fleeting flavours of the finest sake, which is usually consumed chilled.

Fruit-flavoured cocktails are also popular, mostly based on the increasingly fashionable *shochu*, a family of dry vodka-like spirits distilled from ingredients such as potatoes and grains. A highly potent example is Kyushu's *imo-jochu*, which is distilled from sweet potatoes. *Awamori*, a clear Okinawan spirit made exclusively from imported Thai rice, is usually served on the rocks. Starting at 25 percent, it has a deceptive kick. The Japanese drink vast amounts of imported wine, but their own labels are maturing every year. Look out for refreshing, well-structured whites from regions like Tokachi and Yamanashi.

The Japanese are massive consumers of beer, especially German-style lager, which has been produced ever since a German visited Hokkaido in the 1870s and found it ideal for growing hops. The big breweries battle it out in a fiercely

Traditional tea ceremony

More Than Just a Cup of Tea

Nothing expresses Japanese formality and emphasis on social protocol more effectively than the tea ceremony. As you travel around Japan, you might have a chance to participate in a simple tea ceremony at a Zen Buddhist temple in Kamakura or Kyoto, at a teahouse in one of the 'strolling' gardens, or even in special rooms at your hotel.

Although tea drinking appeared early in Japanese history, it was not until the 12th century that the special strain of tea bush and the technique for making powdered green tea (*matcha*) were brought from China. First planted in Uji, near Kyoto, the slightly bitter *matcha* – loaded with caffeine and vitamin C – helped meditating Zen monks to keep their concentration. The drink later became a stimulant of the rich merchant class.

Today's elegant tea ceremony was refined in the 15th century to induce the mental tranquillity necessary to continue along the path towards religious enlightenment. The tea itself was not the point. Rather, the emphasis lay in the protocol, ritual and resulting atmosphere associated with every single aspect of its preparation.

Over the centuries, the ceremony has accumulated exquisitely designed utensils: bowls, tea kettle, tea caddy, hot water jug, miniature brazier, a long, slender scoop for the tea powder and a little whisk for mixing it. A scroll is hung in an alcove, together with an exquisite ikebana flower arrangement.

If you are served first, be sure to bow to the host and then turn to your neighbour and say 'Excuse me for drinking before you'. Take the bowl with your right hand and rest it on the palm of your left, turning the bowl's decorative pattern away from you for others to admire.

Sip the tea loudly, then wipe the bowl's edge and turn its decorative pattern to admire it yourself. Expressing admiration for the tea bowls, utensils and other objects of definitively understated beauty is an important aspect of the proceedings. The ceremony is finished when the host removes the tea caddy and scoop.

competitive market by launching seasonal brews featuring differing flavours and alcohol content (the latter indicated on the side of the can or bottle label).

Finally, the ubiquitous tea. Green tea *(o-cha)* is green because it is unfermented; it was originally introduced from China. The green tea powder is prepared in lukewarm water, and only the finest quality is used in the tea ceremony. *Sencha* is the common variety of tea leaves, while *bancha* (the kind served in sushi bars and small restaurants) is coarser and requires boiling water. Last of all is *hojicha*, a brown tea with a nice smoky tang to it, also brewed using boiling water.

However, many so-called teas actually contain no tea leaves at all. Brewed instead from herbs and grains, they are usually very healthy and served cold in the summer and hot in the winter. Many of the unidentifiable drinks you see in Japanese vending machines are herb or grain teas. To beat the summer heat, try cold *mugi-cha*, made from barley.

Elaborately decorated sake barrels

Western-Style Food

However much you love Japanese food, you might get a craving for something more familiar. The major Western-style hotels have both Western and Japanese menus. In most cities and towns you will find no shortage of establishments claiming to offer such international fare as Indian, French, Italian and Chinese. But be forewarned: such food is usually highly modified to suit the local palate. Anyone used to Chinese food in, say, Hong Kong or even the US is unlikely to be impressed by what is served in Japan. Italian and French fare has become enormously popular, especially among the young, but you should again expect to be disappointed. The dishes you are served might look authentic, but somehow they never taste quite right. (They are also often served in annoyingly small portions.)

As for sandwiches: forget it – except as a last resort. Despite Japan's long record of dramatically improving on imported concepts, the Japanese sandwich is a veritable disaster, with dainty, crustless slices of fluffy white bread providing only a token hint of whatever is supposed to be inside. And at convenience stores, only the truly open-minded will sample such culinary horrors as the fried noodle roll or the fruit salad and whipped cream sandwich.

To Help You Order...

A table for... please	...onegai shimas(u)	...お願いします。
How much is that?	ikura des(u) ka	いくらですか。
The bill, please	o-kanjoo onegai shimas(u)	お勘定、お願いします。
I would like...	... o kudasai	...をください。
fish	sakana	魚
beef	gyuu	牛
pork	buta	豚
chicken	tori	鶏

bread	pan	パン
potatoes	poteto/bareesho	ポテト/馬鈴薯
rice	gohan	ご飯
salad	sarada	サラダ
pickled vegetables	tsukemono	漬物
fruit	kudamono	野菜
vegetables	yasai	果物
pepper	koshoo	コショウ
salt	shio	塩
sugar	satoo	砂糖
water	mizu	水
coffee	koohii	コーヒー
tea	koocha	紅茶
wine	wain	ワイン
beer	biirru	ビール
sake	nihonshu	日本酒

... and Read the Menu

miso soup	miso shiro	みそ汁
grilled fish	yaki zakana	焼き魚
minced beef and vegetables	sukiyaki	すき焼
thin noodles	soba	そば
thick noodles	udon	うどん
cold noodles	hiyamugi	冷麦
noodles in stock with tempura	tempura udon	天ぷらうどん
Chinese noodles in stock	ramen	ラーメン
salted crêpes	okonomiyaki	お好み焼き
tofu	tofou	豆腐
fried pork cutlet	ton katsu	とんかつ
tuna	maguro	鮪/マグロ
salmon	saké	鮭/サケ
prawns	ebi	海老/エビ

HANDY TRAVEL TIPS

An A–Z Summary of Practical Information

A

ACCOMMODATION

A wide variety of accommodation is available in Japan, ranging from international-class Western-style hotels to Buddhist temples. During the Japanese holidays *(see page 236)* early reservations are essential. If you are stuck without a room, contact an office of the Japan Travel Bureau (JNTO), where you will be able to find help.

Western-style hotels. Most of the international hotels belong to the Japan Hotel Association. They are comparable to equivalent hotels in Europe or the US and offer Western-style facilities and cuisine, although Japanese food is also available. Rates may be reduced under certain circumstances (off season, long stay, group discount). Reservations can be made through any travel agent and certain airlines, or by contacting the hotel directly.

Japanese-style inns *(ryokan)*. For a more informal atmosphere and a taste of the Japanese way of life, stay at a traditional inn. These vary from large hotel-scale establishments to small, hospitable, family-run hotels. Reservations can be made through a travel agent or through the inn itself. Prices are always per person (rather than per room) and almost always include a sumptuous dinner and break-

I'd like a single/double room.	**shinguru/daburu ruumu o onegai shimas(u).**	シングル/ダブルルームをお願いします。
I'd like a room with shower/bath.	**basu/shawa tsuki no heya o onegai shimas(u).**	バス/シャワー付の部屋をお願いします。
May I see the room, please?	**heya o misete kudasai?**	部屋を見せてください。

fast featuring regional specialities. Guest rooms are Japanese-style, with *tatami*-mat floors and a cotton *futon* as a bed. En-suite bathrooms are only sometimes available, but most *ryokan* feature private use of a Japanese-style hot tub. The rate is sometimes reduced by 10 percent to 20 percent if meals are omitted, but this should always be agreed before checking in. Check-in time is usually between 3pm and 4pm, check-out time from 10am to 11am. Many *ryokans* also have curfews (usually 11pm) – check when booking.

There are approximately 80,000 *ryokan*, about 2,000 of which belong to the Japan Ryokan Association (www.ryokan.or.jp), who ensure that a high standard of service is maintained. The Japanese Inn Group is a network of independent and very reasonably priced *ryokan* providing a warm and friendly way to experience Japanese-style lodging.

Guesthouses (minshuku). This is another type of Japanese-style accommodation, often located in holiday resorts. The guest is treated as a member of the family. The per-person charge only sometimes includes dinner and breakfast, and you are expected to lay out your bedding at night and roll it up and stow it away again the next morning.

The Japan National Tourist Organisation (JNTO) recommends about 300 *minshuku* for foreign visitors. Welcome Inn Reservation Centre offers a free reservation service at a wide range of *minshuku* and *ryokan* that charge not more than ¥8,000 per single room or ¥13,000 per double room per night. Reservation request forms are available at JNTO overseas offices. Note that the Welcome Inn service now strictly requires reservations at least three weeks in advance. Highly recommended and much more flexible are the 70 member inns of the Japanese Inn Group (Reservation Centre, 1-19-16 Utsubohonmachi, Nishi-ku, Osaka, tel: 06-6444-6740, fax: 06-6444-6750, email: info@jpinn.com, www.jpinn.com; or c/o International Tourism Centre of Japan, Kanda Urban building 9F, 2-4-2

Kandatsukasa-cho, Chiyoda-ku, Tokyo 101-0048, tel: (03) 3252-1717, fax: (03) 3252-1521).

Home-stay system. If you want to learn more about typical Japanese home life first-hand, you can stay with a Japanese family by applying to the Japanese Association of the Experiment in International Living (EIL Japan), which organises stays of one to four weeks. You need to apply to an EIL office six to eight weeks in advance of your planned stay. In the UK, contact the EIL, 287 Worcester Road, Malvern, Worcestershire WR14 4EN; tel: (01684) 562577, fax: (01684) 562212, www.eiluk.org. In the US, contact World Learning, P.O. Box 676, Brattleboro, VT 05302; tel: 802-257-7751; fax: 802-258-3428; www.world learning.org.

Buddhist temples (shukubo). Anyone may stay at one of the many Japanese temples offering surprisingly luxurious accommodation, in the tradition of temples offering accommodation to wandering pilgrims. These provide a glimpse into the monks' daily life and routines. Food is usually strictly vegetarian and even sumptuous. Guests at the temples are sometimes expected to help with some light chores and may attend early morning prayer services. Reservations can be made through the JNTO, which can provide full details. The greatest concentration of shukubo is in the mountain-top Buddhist enclave of Koyasan, in Wakayama (see www.shukubo.jp), and Kyoto.

Youth hostels. Anyone – whether a member or not – may stay at the public youth hostels run by regional governments. All that's needed is a passport or ID card. To stay at a privately run hostel, you need a valid Youth Hostels Association membership card or an International Guest Card obtainable from Japan Youth Hostels, Inc. Reservations should be made directly to individual hostels (if possible in writing) or by phone, stating name, address, sex, membership card number, length of stay, arrival and departure dates, and meal requirements for the day you arrive. Booking forms are available from the International Youth Hostels Federation.

For further information, contact Japan Youth Hostels: Kanda Amerex Building 9F, 3-1-16, Misaki-cho, Chiyoda-ku, Tokyo 100-0006; tel: (03) 3288-1417; fax: (03) 3288-1248; www.jyh. or.jp/english.

AIRPORTS

Tokyo's airport at Narita and Kansai International Airport near Osaka are Japan's two main air gateways. However, there are also international airports at Nagoya, Fukuoka and Okinawa, and a few international flights use Hiroshima, Oita, Okayama, Kagoshima, Kumamoto, Nagasaki, Komatsu, Kanazawa, Niigata, Sendai, Takamatsu and Sapporo airports.

Narita. New Tokyo International Airport (Narita; www.narita-airport.jp/en) is almost 60 km (37 miles) east of the city centre. Access to Tokyo is by limousine, bus, train or taxi; tickets for all downtown transfers can be purchased in the airport arrival lobby. Buses depart at frequent intervals for the Tokyo City Air Terminal and numerous other major points around Tokyo (travel time around 60 minutes) and Yokohama (90 minutes). Travel time is heavily dependent on traffic conditions. If you have a meeting or a flight to catch, assume the worst and allow plenty of extra time for traffic. The bus has long been the standard airport link; only the fattest expense accounts can bear the cost of the trip to or from Tokyo in a Japanese taxi. There is also a bus link with Haneda, Tokyo's main domestic airport, taking around 75 minutes.

Various trains are also available, operated by Japan Railways (JR) and Keisei Railways. These are faster and more reliable, since they avoid Tokyo's notorious traffic. All services take 60 to 90 minutes to or from central Tokyo depending on the service. In Narita, the train platforms are located underground below the terminal buildings. The JR Narita Express (also known as N'EX) goes to Shinjuku, Shibuya, Ikebukuro, Ofuna and Yokohama via Tokyo Station. The less-expensive Keisei Skyliner Train leaves from the Keisei station in Ueno and arrives at the Keisei Airport Station (just six minutes from the airport by shuttle bus). Finally, an Airport Limited Express train service links Narita with Haneda Airport; that journey takes about one hour 45 minutes.

A taxi from Narita to the centre of Tokyo can take 90 minutes or more, depending on the traffic conditions. An inter-airport transfer to Tokyo Haneda Airport by limousine bus takes one hour 40 minutes.

Haneda. Tokyo Haneda (www.tokyo-airport-bldg.co.jp/en) is the city's second airport, serving mainly domestic routes. It is 20km (12½ miles) south of the city centre. Transport to town is by monorail to Hamamatsu-cho Station (departure every six minutes, travel time 15 minutes).

Kansai. Kansai International Airport (Osaka; www.kansai-airport.or.jp/en) is situated southeast of the city centre on Osaka Bay. A comprehensive network of limousine buses leave every 20 minutes or so from main points around Osaka (travel time around 45 minutes), including Umeda and Namba stations, as well as from Kobe, Nara and other locations throughout Kansai. You can also take the Nankai 'RAPIT' express train from the Nankai station in Namba, the JR Airport Express from Kyobashi, or JR's Haruka express train from Kyoto.

Central Japan International Airport, or Centrair, was built specially for the Aichi Expo 2005 on reclaimed land in Ise Bay, 35km (22 miles) from Nagoya. You can reach Nagoya by train in under

30 minutes using the Shinkansen, JR Line, Kintetsu Line and subway. Airport buses leave regularly from the 1st floor of the Passenger Terminal Building.

B

BATHHOUSES

Whether you're at a hot spring resort, a local *sento* (bathhouse) or a traditional inn, the procedure is the same. Disrobe, enter the bathroom (in public you hide your modesty with a small flannel), and wash and rinse off thoroughly under a shower before easing into the hot bath – which is for soaking, rather than washing yourself. Don't pull the plug after you've finished: others will use the same water.

BUDGETING FOR YOUR TRIP

To give you an idea of what to expect, here is a list of average prices in Japanese yen (¥). However, they can only be approximate, as inflation creeps relentlessly higher here as elsewhere. A consumption tax of five percent is added to most goods and services.

Airport transfer. Narita to Tokyo City Air Terminal: ¥2,900. Narita to JR Tokyo Station by N'EX: ¥2,940. Narita to Keisei Ueno Station (Skyliner train): ¥l,920. Narita to Haneda Airport (limousine bus): ¥3,000. Narita to Yokohama City Air Terminal (limousine bus): ¥3,500.

Car hire (rental). Average daily rates with unlimited mileage: economy: ¥5,000–9,000; compact: ¥9,000–14,000; mid-size: ¥14,000–¥30,000; full-size: ¥29,500–31,000. Weekly and monthly rates are also available.

Cigarettes. Japanese brands ¥220–260; imported ¥300–330.

Guides. ¥12,000–80,000 per day (half-day rates are also available).

Barbers and hairdressers. Hotels: haircut ¥6,000; shave ¥3,000; shampoo ¥5,000.

Hotels (double room with private bath). Western-style, per room: ¥10,000–45,000 daily. *Ryokan* (including two meals, per person): ¥10,000–40,000 daily (rates often vary for busy and off-peak seasons). *Minshuku* (including two meals): ¥5,000–8,000 daily.

Meals. In a moderately priced restaurant, a Western meal will cost from ¥2,000–5,000 (steak dishes tend to be more expensive than others), and a Japanese meal will cost between ¥1,500 and ¥4,000, although expect to pay a great deal more for *kaiseki ryori*, Japan's refined, seasonally modulated cuisine. Lunch set specials in the ¥1,500–2,000 range can be very good deals.

Nightclubs. In most nightclubs there's a cover charge (¥3,000 and up). Should you find yourself in a hostess bar you can expect to pay anything from ¥5,000 to ¥60,000 for two hours, plus service and tax, which means an evening's entertainment can cost as much as ¥130,000.

Taxi. Fares in Tokyo start at ¥710 for the first 2km (1¼ miles); elsewhere in Japan base fares begin at ¥680, but vary according to region. Add ¥80 for each additional 247m (299yds), plus a time charge if the taxi is moving at less than 10km/h (6mph). From 11pm to 5am the fare is increased by 30 percent.

Public transport. *Bus:* in Tokyo the single fare on all routes is ¥210; in other towns a flat rate of ¥160–260 is charged on most routes. For longer journeys the fare is calculated depending on the distance travelled. Long-distance coach: Tokyo–Nagoya (6hr)

¥6,420; Tokyo–Kyoto (8hr) ¥6,000; Tokyo–Osaka (8hr 45min) ¥6,000. *Subway:* Tokyo minimum fare ¥130, Osaka ¥200. *Train:* The Japan Rail Pass offers non-residents unlimited national rail travel on most of the JR and Shinkansen network. A first class (or 'green') rail pass is ¥37,800 for seven days, ¥61,200 for 14 days, ¥79,600 for 21 days. An ordinary-class rail pass is ¥28,300 for seven days, ¥45,100 for 14 days and ¥57,700 for 21 days.

C

CAMPING

There are a number of camping sites throughout the country. For more information, contact the Japan Auto Camping Association (New Ueno Building, 7th floor, 1-24 Yotsuya, Shinjuku-ku, Tokyo 160-0008; tel: 03-3357-2851, fax: 03-3357-2850). The Tourist Information Centres (TIC) in Tokyo (Yurakucho) and Kyoto (in the Kyoto Tower) provide details of reservations and costs and can supply a map of Japan showing the camping sites. Camping on private land is sometimes possible, but you must obtain prior permission from the owner.

Experienced campers might want to stay in the public lodgings *(kokumin shukusha)* built in scenic places or national park areas and operated by the Ministry of Health and Welfare. Lodging includes two meals. Reservations should be made directly with the lodging.

CAR HIRE (RENTAL)

There are car hire firms in all the major cities. Numerous local firms vie with well-known international companies, keeping prices competitive. Except for French, German and Swiss drivers, who only require an official translation of their licences, an International Driving Permit is required. It is possible to hire a car with an English-speaking driver, either through your hotel or a travel agent.

CLIMATE

Japan has four dramatically distinct seasons – although many Japanese feel the rainy season lasting from mid-June to early July should also be counted. There is a vast difference between the subarctic north and the subtropical south, and the climate varies considerably according to region and season.

January and February are the ideal months for winter sports, when most of the country north of Osaka lies under a blanket of snow. March, April and May are cherry blossom time: warm and sunny. From mid-June to mid-July is the rainy season, followed by hot, jungle-like humidity during August and September. Unless you enjoy your clothes sticking to you from dawn till dusk, this is a good time to avoid Japan, since walking around is essential for sightseeing. September usually brings strong winds, more rain and typhoons, followed by clear skies and bright sunshine during the autumn months.

Weather is definitely a popular and ongoing topic of conversation throughout the year, especially the rain, which can be unpredictable much of the time. For this reason, a sturdy collapsible umbrella is an essential accessory for the savvy traveller in Japan. Japan's monthly average daytime temperatures in degrees Celsius are:

	J	F	M	A	M	J	J	A	S	O	N	D
Max °C	16	16	18	21	23	26	28	28	27	24	21	18
Min °C	-4	-3	0	6	12	16	20	22	17	11	4	-1

CLOTHING

Most Japanese have conservative tastes in clothing. Dress is slowly changing both in the workplace and in social settings (but most businessmen still wear dark suits, white shirts and ill-fitting shoes). As a result, subdued colours and subtle designs are preferable – at least if you don't want to stand out too much.

Your wardrobe should be versatile, lightweight and easy to wash. Be sure to pack a raincoat. Extra-warm sweaters and a warm coat are necessary in winter. You should avoid tight, restrictive clothing: remember that you will often be seated at low tables with your legs folded underneath you or crossed – not easy in a tight skirt. Remember also that your socks will often be on view and you'll be embarrassed if your toes are poking through holes for all to see; temple floors can be very cold, so pack at least one pair of thick woolly socks. You will have to take your shoes off so often that you will be glad to wear slip-ons. A good pair of comfortable walking shoes is useful for sightseeing, as Japanese paths are gravelled and hard.

If you want to buy clothes in Japan, be forewarned that both men's and women's clothing is designed for Japanese body shapes, which are different from those of most Westerners. Also, Japanese underwear generally does not suit Western builds. However, Western-sized clothes are gradually becoming more available in Tokyo and other major cities.

CRIME AND SAFETY (see also POLICE)

As the crime rate in Japan is relatively low, it is unlikely that you will be attacked or robbed. However, Japan's is by no means a crime-free society, and all categories of crime – including sexual assault and other violent crimes – are rising steadily. As when travelling anywhere in the world, sensible precautions are recommended. In Tokyo and other large cities, small neighbourhood police boxes (called *koban*, easily identifiable with their large red lamp above the door) are located at most major street junctions.

CUSTOMS AND ENTRY REQUIREMENTS

To enter Japan, you will need a valid passport, and you will have to fill in an embarkation/disembarkation card. On arrival you may be asked to show your return ticket and prove you have the means to support yourself during your stay.

Visas. Tourists from the UK and Ireland do not need a visa if they intend to stay less than 180 days in Japan. Americans, Canadians, Australians and New Zealanders may stay 90 days without a visa. Tourists from South Africa must obtain a visa from a Japanese embassy before leaving home. Any visitor staying more than 90 days must apply at the local Japanese police station or city hall for an Alien Registration Certificate.

Customs regulations. Officially, goods you bring into Japan should be declared either orally or in writing. However, Japan has now adopted the customs clearance system of spot-checking practised in many other countries. There is no limit on the amount of currency you can bring into or take out of the country. However, if you want to take out more than ¥1,000,000 you are required to report this to customs. Certain fresh fruits and vegetables may not be imported into Japan. Certain stimulants found in Western medicines are prohibited as well.

Nothing to declare. **menzee no han-i nai shika arimasen.** 免税の範囲内しかありません。

D

DRIVING

The difficulties of driving in Japan shouldn't be underestimated. Driving standards vary greatly, and Japanese roads seem to have more than their fair share of speed demons and people with zero observation skills. As a result, traffic accidents, injuries and fatalities keep breaking records. For visitors, defensive and cautious driving is essential.

Traffic keeps to the left – which won't worry British drivers – but almost all visitors from abroad will find the traffic conditions daunting. The streets are congested, and parking is highly restricted. The greatest challenge to navigating is the fact that very few streets have names. Instead, building blocks are numbered based on an archaic system; most streets simply serve to separate the blocks. Most traffic signs are written in both roman and Japanese characters.

Speed limits are 40km/h (25mph) in towns, 60km/h (38mph) in suburbs and 100km/h (63mph) on expressways.

The Japanese Automobile Federation (emergency tel: 0570-00-8139; www.jaf.or.jp/e) publishes an English-language guide to driving in Japan entitled *Rules of the Road*. Japan's drink-driving laws are very severe – the legal limit is zero – but drinking is so commonplace and traffic police so few and far between that late-night driving in cities should be avoided when at all possible.

E

ELECTRICITY

The current is 100 volts throughout Japan, with 50 cycles in Tokyo and eastern Japan and 60 cycles in western Japan (including Nagoya, Kyoto and Osaka). However, most modern appliances are designed to handle both, so this discrepancy is rarely a problem. American-style flat-pin plugs and outlets are used; non-Americans wishing to use their own appliances will need an adapter and, if necessary, a transformer. Major hotels have 110- and 220-volt outlets for razors, hairdryers and other appliances.

EMBASSIES

Australia: 2-1-14 Mita, Minato-ku, Tokyo 108-8361; tel: (03) 5232-4111, fax: (03) 5232-4149; www.australia.or.jp/english/seifu.
Canada: 7-3-38 Akasaka, Minato-ku, Tokyo 107-8503; tel: (03) 5412-6200, fax: (03) 5412-6247; www.canadanet.or.jp.
New Zealand: 20-40 Kamiyama-cho, Shibuya-ku, Tokyo 150-0047; tel: (03) 3467-2271, fax: (03) 3467-2278; www.nzembassy.com/japan.

UK: 1 Ichiban-cho, Chiyoda-ku, Tokyo 102-8381; tel: (03) 5211-1100, fax: (03) 5275-3164; www.uknow.or.jp/be_e.
US: 1-10-5 Akasaka, Minato-ku, Tokyo 107-8420; tel: (03) 3224-5000, fax: (03) 3505-1862; http://tokyo.usembassy.gov.

EMERGENCIES

In case of illness, you should notify the hotel desk immediately. For hospital information in Tokyo, in English, call (03) 5285-8181 (daily 9am–8pm).

Emergency telephone numbers are as follows:
Police: 110
Fire: 119
Ambulance: 119

Call the police!	**keesatsu o yonde**	警察を呼んで！
Find a doctor!	**isha o yonde**	医者を呼んで！
Help!	**tas(u)kete**	助けて！
I'm lost.	**michi ni mayoi mash(i)ta**	道に迷いました。

ETIQUETTE

There are points of etiquette for doing just about everything in Japan (blowing your nose in public for instance, especially at high volume is considered rude). Although as a visitor you may be blissfully un-aware of most of them, the cardinal rule is to try to be courteous at all times. This will cover a multitude of sins, and the sentiment you express will invariably be reciprocated.

At work and in most formal situations, the Japanese may seem reticent and lacking in spontaneity. But when drinking and having a good time, Japanese, especially the men, can become very raucous and often let out their real opinions and feelings. It is often said that 'the Japanese are only polite with their shoes off', which means that they are polite and courteous with people they know well and would be indoors with (where shoes are always removed).

Foreigners are usually forgiven for any breach of etiquette, so there's no need to spend time worrying about what is right and wrong. Japanese behaviour in general is situational, and the Japanese themselves often do not know the right thing to do in any given situation. 'It all depends on the situation,' remarks the smart alec, but it's often fun for everyone involved when one of 'us' makes a slip. Sometimes it actually helps to break the ice and put everyone in a more relaxed mood.

Bowing. The custom of bowing has, in many cases, become somewhat of a conditioned reflex. Foreigners, in general, are not expected to bow, and this is especially evident if a Japanese person first reaches out to shake hands.

Drinking. When having beer or sake, one always pours for the other party, who will hold up the glass while it is filled. It is polite to keep the glasses filled; if you have had enough, leave your glass full.

Eating. Soup is sipped directly from the bowl in which it is served. So is the broth of hot noodles, except for *ramen*, which comes with a spoon. When sipping soup, tea or other hot liquids, it is customary to draw in a good amount of air at the same time. Slurping sounds for noodles and other soup dishes are quite acceptable, but should be kept to a minimum in polite company.

Footwear. There is a strong distinction in Japan between the areas inside and outside the home. Just inside the entrance to homes (and many restaurants) is an area where you are expected to remove your shoes. From here, you step up into the living area either wearing the slippers provided or in your stockinged feet. This keeps the house clean and increases the amount of useable space, since you can sit on the floor without worrying about getting dirty. (Men usually sit cross-legged and women sit with their legs tucked under.) Slippers are never worn on tatami mats. Go barefoot instead.

The toilet, however, is one area of the house that is considered 'dirty', so separate slippers are provided for use in there.

Invitations. It is rare to be invited to someone's home. Most people live too far out of town or find their homes too cramped to invite guests. If you receive an invitation, take along a small gift with you: flowers or a food item are common gifts, or perhaps something from your own country.

G

GAY AND LESBIAN TRAVELLERS

Japan is not particularly hostile to homosexuality, although it is not asserted or celebrated as openly as it is in some Western cultures. Visitors might find the gay and lesbian nightlife scene a little difficult to discover and negotiate. The best-known quarter in Tokyo is Shinjuku 2-chome, but there are clubs, discos and drag bars in Roppongi and other areas as well. *Tokyo Journal,* the capital's English-language quarterly magazine, includes some gay and lesbian listings.

GETTING THERE

From the UK. Daily flights depart to Tokyo and Kansai from London's Heathrow and Gatwick airports. Nonstop flights take about 12 hours.

From North America. There are several daily nonstop flights from New York, Los Angeles, San Francisco and many other cities. Round-the-world fares are available, which allow flights first to Europe and then on to the East Asia, returning directly to North America. This fare is designed for those who wish to stop en route in Europe.

From Australia. Direct flights run daily from Sydney to Tokyo, taking about 9 hours.

GUIDES AND TOURS

To help visitors, the Japan National Tourist Organisation (JNTO) has inaugurated a 'goodwill guide' service. These voluntary guides – there are more than 35,000 of them – can easily be recognised by the distinctive badges they wear. They are happy to answer questions, give directions and assist in any other way they can.

If you need the services of a professional guide for sightseeing, shopping or business purposes, you can arrange for one through major travel agents or the Japan Guide Association (Shin-Kokusai Bldg, 3-4-1 Marunouchi, Chiyoda-ku, Tokyo 100-0005; tel: (03) 3213-2706; www.jga21c.or.jp). This organisation can provide guides who speak English, French, Italian, Spanish, Portuguese, German, Russian, Chinese, or Korean.

A popular and reasonably priced option with visitors to Tokyo is to take a bus tour of the city's main sights. Options include half-day, full-day and evening tours. Prices range from ¥3,300 for a morning tour to around ¥12,000 for an eight-hour trip including a river cruise.

English-language tours can be booked from major hotels in downtown Tokyo or directly with the tour company. Companies offering bus tours include Hato Bus Tokyo (tel: 03-3435-6081; www.hatobus.com/en); Japan Gray Line Company (tel: 03-3433-5745; www.jgl.co.jp/inbound); and Sunrise Tours (tel: 03-5796 5454; www.jtbgmt.com/sunrisetour).

H

HEALTH AND MEDICAL CARE

In general, levels of hygiene are very high, and it is very unlikely that you will become ill as a result of eating or drinking something.

The tap water, though heavily chlorinated, is drinkable. Most food is of a high standard.

For minor ailments, your hotel or local Tourist Information Centre (TIC) can contact an English-speaking doctor. Hospitals with English-speaking staff include St Luke's International Hospital, the International Catholic Hospital and the International Medical Center of Japan in Tokyo; the Bluff Hospital in Yokohama; the Japan Baptist Hospital and the Kyoto City Hospital in Kyoto; the Sumitomo Hospital and the Yodogawa Christian Hospital in Osaka; and the Kobe Kaisei Hospital and the Kobe Adventist Hospital in Kobe. For hospital information in Tokyo, dial (03) 5285-8181.

Although you will find a large selection of imported medicines and toiletries at the American Pharmacy in Tokyo (Hibiya Park Bldg. 1, 1-8-1 Yurakucho, Chiyoda-ku; tel: (03) 3271-4034/5), they are much more expensive than back home. If you have special medical needs, it's best to bring an ample supply with you. Japanese pharmacies are called *yakkyoku*; you might also notice *kampoy-akkyoku*, which sell traditional herbal remedies.

For urgent dental treatment, go to Arisugawa Parkside Dental Office, Arisugawa Residence, 5-14-1 Minami-Azabu, Suite B-104, Minato-ku, Tokyo 106-0047, tel: (03) 5475-3312, fax: (03) 5475-3313.

HOLIDAYS

On the following holidays, banks and offices will be closed, but shops and restaurants are unaffected. The exception is the New Year period, from 30 December to 3 January, when virtually everything shuts down. Note also that when a holiday falls on a Sunday, the Monday after is also observed as a holiday.

1 January	*New Year's Day*
2nd Monday in January	*Coming of Age Day*
11 February	*National Foundation Day*
20/21 March	*Vernal Equinox Day*
29 April	*Greenery Day*

3 May	Constitution Day
4 May	'Between Day'
5 May	Children's Day
3rd Monday in July	Marine Day
3rd Monday in September	Respect for the Aged Day
23 or 24 September	Autumnal Equinox
2nd Monday in October	Health and Sports Day
3 November	Culture Day
23 November	Labour Thanksgiving Day
23 December	Emperor Akihito's Birthday

If you intend to be in Japan during New Year, Golden Week (29 April to 5 May and adjacent weekends) or the school holidays (March–April and July–August), make your reservations well in advance, as hotels will be full and public transport more packed than ever. But these periods might be ideal times to visit Tokyo under less crowded conditions – except at New Year, when thousands of provincials flock to the Imperial Palace gardens.

L

LANGUAGE

Unless you already speak good Japanese, it's best to stick to English. It might be fun to exchange a few words or phrases in Japanese for 'Thank you', 'How are you?' or 'Good-bye'. But if you give the impression that you're able to take on a fully fledged conversation, you're likely to be swept away by a torrent of incomprehensible syllables instead of the simple communication you really wanted.

Speak slowly and clearly in English. Try to avoid unnecessary expressions and figures of speech, and instead use the simplest grammar to phrase your questions and answers. The Berlitz phrase book, *Japanese for Travellers*, will help you in situations where you need to speak some Japanese.

The following are some useful Japanese words and expressions:

Good morning	**ohayoo gozaimas(u)**	おはようございます。
Hello/Good afternoon	**kon-nichi-wa**	こんにちは。
Good evening	**konban wa**	こんばんは。
Good night	**oyasumi nasai**	おやすみなさい。
Goodbye	**sayoonara**	さようなら。
Please	**doozo/onegai shimas(u)**	どうぞ。/お願いします。
Thank you	**arigatoo**	ありがとう。
My pleasure	**doozo**	どうぞ。
Yes/No	**hai/iie**	はい。/いいえ。
Excuse me	**sumimasen**	すみません。
I don't understand	**wakarimasen**	分かりません。
How much?	**ikura des(u) ka**	いくらですか。

Numbers

one	**ichi**	一
two	**ni**	二
three	**san**	三
four	**shi/yon**	四
five	**go**	五
six	**roku**	六
seven	**schichi/nana**	七
eight	**hachi**	八
nine	**kyuu/ku**	九
ten	**juu**	十
twenty	**ni-juu**	二十
thirty	**san-juu**	三十
one hundred	**hyaku**	百
one thousand	**sen**	千

LEFT LUGGAGE

Carry as little luggage as possible when travelling in Japan. Trains and stations, especially, are not designed for travellers with more than a small overnight bag. If you're thinking of making all your Tokyo train and subway connections while hauling several large bags – forget it. The train/subway map looks neat and tidy, but station connections are serious hikes with no carts or porters available, and seemingly endless stairs. Hotels, of course, will usually store luggage for guests heading off on adventures.

The international airports have checkrooms, although for security reasons there are no coin lockers. Most train and subway stations have coin lockers of varying sizes. Time limit is three days. After that, contents are removed. Checkrooms for large bags are located at several main JR stations. Luggage can be stored for up to two weeks.

M

MAPS

The JNTO provides free tourist maps of Japan, Tokyo, Kyoto/Nara, Fuji, Osaka and Hokkaido, as well as maps (including location maps) to hotels, *ryokan,* hostels and railways. All of these are available in English. A road map of Japan, published in English by Buyodo Co., can be found in main bookshops.

MEDIA

Foreign-language magazines, newspapers and books can be found in large bookshops and hotels. Several interesting English-language magazines are published in Japan. These tend to fall into two categories: events magazines and those focusing on Japanese culture. Of the first group, look out for the quarterly *Tokyo Journal*, the city's oldest events magazine, *JSelect* and *Metropolis*, a free weekly. *Kansai Time Out* and *Kansai Scene* cover the western region of Japan. *J@pan.Inc* is an internet- and business-related quarterly magazine.

Several on-line magazines are also up and running: *Tokyo Q* (www.tokyoq.com) is the unquestionable leader, with the best restaurant and nightlife postings, followed by www.bento.com, a food guide. *Superfuture* (www.superfuture.com) is a trendy site for shopping, restaurants, bars and forthcoming events. If you would like to research costs before going to Japan, check out the thorough and extensive www.pricechecktokyo.com.

Readers of English are blessed with three daily newspapers published by Japanese media: the *Japan Times* is the best of the crop with both syndicated articles and interesting pieces by Japan-based journalists, followed by the *Daily Yomiuri*, and the financial paper *Nihon Keizai Shimbun*. There is also an English *Nikkei Weekly*. Travellers will find them useful for their coverage of local news, features and events, and for the advertisements. Monday's edition of the *Japan Times* is the place to find help-wanted ads, half of them for English teachers (and a few for French or German) and the rest for everyone else. These papers can be purchased at most newsstand kiosks on the street and in train and subway stations. Also found frequently at kiosks is the *International Herald Tribune*, with an *Asahi Shimbun* back supplement, and the *Asian Wall Street Journal*. Other foreign newspapers can be found at most hotels and at the larger bookshops.

Television programmes are mostly in Japanese, although news and foreign films are broadcast bilingually on TV sets. Major hotels have satellite TV and English-language cable stations such as CNN.

MONEY

The monetary system is based on the Japanese yen (¥). Coins come in denominations of ¥1, ¥5, ¥10, ¥50, ¥100 and ¥500; banknotes are in ¥1,000, ¥2,000, ¥5,000 and ¥10,000 bills. The

¥10 and ¥100 coins are useful for public phones, ¥50 and ¥100 coins for bus tickets, vending machines and short-distance railway tickets.

Currency exchange. International hotels will change either traveller's cheques or foreign currency (if exchange quotations are available) into yen. Accredited banks, of course will do the same – at slightly better rates. Stores in many tourist areas are increasingly able to accept payment in currencies other than yen; you will need to present your passport.

When you enter a bank, an employee might greet you and show you the appropriate window. If not, simply look for the relevant sign. You will be invited to sit down while the transaction is being completed, which can take 15 minutes or longer; your name will be called when your money is ready.

Most banks have a special foreign-exchange section, where you can change foreign currency and traveller's cheques for yen (you must present your passport).

ATMs and credit cards. Despite Japan's financial sophistication, there are very few places where you can use an international credit card and PIN number to make spot cash withdrawals, although most post offices should have ATMs that accept international credit cards. Since the streets are so safe, however, you can simply take as much cash with you each day as you expect to need for incidentals.

For larger expenditures, Visa, American Express and Master-Card are widely accepted in hotels, inns, restaurants and shops. Traveller's cheques are not.

Tax refunds. A consumption tax of 5 percent will be added to all purchases, but department stores have special tax refund programmes for foreign visitors on large purchases, usually over

¥10,000. Some stores limit this refund to clothing only. Check at the information desk – usually located on the first floor near the main entrance – before making a purchase. You will need to show your passport for a tax exemption.

I'd like to change some money.	**o-kane o kaetain des(u) ga.**	お金を替えたいんですが。
I'd like to change some travellers' cheques.	**toraberaazu chekku o kankin sh(i)tain des(u) ga.**	トラベラーズチェックを換金したいんですが。
Where are the cash machines?	**kyasshu koonaa wa doko des(u) ka.**	キャッシュコーナーはどこですか。

◯

OPENING HOURS

Banks: Open 9am–3pm weekdays; closed on Saturday and Sunday.

Government offices: Open 9am–5pm weekdays; closed Saturday and Sunday.

Post offices: Main post offices open 9am–7pm weekdays, Saturday 9am–3pm or 5pm; closed on Sunday.

Barbers and hairdressers: Open 9am–8pm daily except closing days (usually Monday for barbers, Tuesday for hairdressers).

Museums: Open 9am–5pm (last admission 4.30pm) daily except Monday. Most museums are open 9am–5pm on Sunday and national holidays.

Shops: Most shops open 10am–8pm every day. Department stores are open 10am–8pm weekdays (until 6.30pm or 7pm on Saturday, Sunday and holidays); they usually close for one day during the week.

Temples: Open 8am or 9am to 4.30pm in summer and until 4pm in the winter.

P

PHOTOGRAPHY

Although there are no restrictions on what you can photograph, use your discretion in religious places. Virtually every Japanese is an avid amateur photographer so camera stores are plentiful everywhere. All popular types of film, discs, cards, batteries and general accessories are widely available.

POLICE

Dial **110** for immediate police assistance or emergencies. There are small police stations or booths *(koban)* on most busy street corners. The police wear a dark blue uniform with a peaked cap. They are extremely courteous and will be ready to help you at any time. You should always present your passport when dealing with the police.

I've lost my…	…o nak(u)shi mash(i)ta	…をなくしました。
wallet/handbag/ passport	saifu/handobaggu/ pas(u)pooto	財布/ハンドバッグ/ パスポート

POST OFFICES

Main post offices are open Mon–Fri 9am–7pm, Sat 9am–3pm or 5pm and closed on Sun. Local and branch offices are open Mon–Fri 9am–5pm and closed on Saturdays and Sundays.

Stamps are sold at post offices and hotels, as well as at some tobacconists and pharmacies. Mail boxes (red for domestic mail, blue for overseas and express mail) are placed on street corners. Some mail boxes have two slots (for domestic and express/international); if you're not sure which to use, either will do. You can also mail letters at hotel desks.

An airmail letter from Japan to any destination in Europe, North America or Oceania is ¥110 (for 10 ounces or less); the rate for a postcard to any place in the world is ¥70. The postal service is fast and reliable.

PUBLIC TRANSPORT

Taxis. These are plentiful and readily available at hotels, stations, or airports. Cabs can be flagged down at street corners except in certain locations (such as the Ginza), where they stop only at taxi ranks. They are bright yellow or green and have a lamp on the roof. If the light in the bottom right-hand corner of the windscreen is red, the taxi is vacant; if it's green, it is occupied. The rear doors are remotely controlled by the driver; don't open and close them yourself.

Few taxi drivers speak English, so have your destination written down on a piece of paper. After 11pm there is a 30 percent surcharge. However, many taxi drivers in Tokyo prefer more lucrative late-night fares than hotel-bound foreigners and might not stop. If you have a problem, ask a Japanese to hail a taxi for you. There is no need to tip taxi drivers.

Subway. The subway lines in Japanese cities are usually colour-coded and easy to use. Trains are frequent, clean and safe; they run until around midnight. To buy your ticket from the vending machine, first insert coins or notes, then press the button with the fare corresponding to your destination station. If necessary, select another train line that you will change onto, and the fare buttons will change accordingly. Insert your ticket in the automatic ticket barrier, then walk through and pick up your ticket on the other side.

You can buy one-day 'open' tickets, which give a day's unlimited travel on the local subways, or (for slightly more) 'combination tickets' valid for all trains, subways and buses. Station platform signs are in Japanese and English; the smaller print at the bottom of the sign indicates the previous and following stations. Avoid the rush-hour periods (7am–9am and 5pm–7pm), when trains and subways are sometimes packed to more than three times their specified capacity. If you do travel during rush-hour, expect to be pushed and bumped around; there's no need to be polite – just push along with everyone else.

Bus. A complex network of buses connects most areas of the large cities (in Tokyo it's generally easier to take the subway). Although the destination of the bus is usually written in Japanese only, in Kyoto and Nara there are recorded announcements in English at important stops. In Tokyo you board at the front of the bus and pay using the driver's machine as you get on. Elsewhere you take a ticket from the machine at the rear door when you board, and pay when you get off. Carry some ¥10 and ¥100 coins with you, although the fare machines usually give change for ¥1,000 notes.

Trains. The Japan Railways (JR; www.japanrail.com) network covers the whole country; the trains are clean, safe and astonishingly punctual. Other private railway networks serve specific regions and are just as much a part of the transport landscape as JR. (Interestingly, JR trains are often the most expensive and the least comfortable, so always investigate alternative lines in your intended direction.)

JR's world-famous *shinkansen* bullet train has several lines. The fastest *(nozomi)* utilise the newest equipment, and are capable of a white-knuckle 300km/h (188mph) speed, although the official speed limit is 270km/h (168mph). First-class carriages are called 'green cars' *(greensha)* and are designated by a green four-leaf clover symbol. Most visitors to Japan will benefit hugely from the Japan Railpass (www.japanrailpass.net), which provides unlimited travel throughout Japan on JR trains (except the *nozomi* super-express bullet train), buses and the Miyajima ferry. These passes must be bought before arriving in Japan, from Japan Air Lines, JNTO offices or travel agents. For more information about the Japan Railpass, see BUDGETING FOR YOUR TRIP.

Air travel. Three main airlines provide extensive regular services connecting the various cities and islands of Japan. The following airlines have toll-free, English-speaking agents and updated websites for information and reservations. These numbers can only be dialled in Japan.

Japan Air Lines (JAL): tel: 0120-25-5971; www.jal.co.jp/en
All Nippon Airways (ANA): tel: 0120-029709; www.ana.co.jp/eng

Where can I get a taxi?	tak(u)shii wa doko de nore mas(u) ka	タクシーはどこで乗れますか。
How much will the journey cost?	ikura ni narimas(u) ka	いくらになりますか。
How do I get back to the station?	eki niwaa doo yatte ikemas(u) ka	駅には、どうやって行けますか。
Where's the ticket office?	kippu uriba wa dokko des(u) ka	きっぷうりばはどこですか。
single/ return	katamichi/ ookufu	片道/往復

R

RELIGION

Although Shinto and Buddhism are the major religions, there are over 1,400,000 Christians in Japan, with churches in most towns. However, few services are in English. For the times of Protestant, Catholic, Greek and Russian Orthodox, Muslim and Jewish services, look at the English-language newspapers or inquire at the local Tourist Information Centre.

T

TELEPHONES

For calls originating abroad, first dial the country code for Japan (81), and then the specific city code (Tokyo is 3, Osaka is 6, Yokohama is 45, Kyoto is 75). If you are calling from one Japanese city to another, you must add a 0 before the city code.

Public telephones are differentiated by colour and size; all can be used for local, intercity, or long-distance calls. Green phones are generally used for domestic calls, although some can also be used for international ones, and accept coins and phonecards. Grey phones marked 'ISDN/International & Domestic Card/Coin Telephone' can be used for direct calls.

For domestic calls, NTT phonecards are available from convenience stores, machines and many shops. Cards are much more convenient than coins, especially since the telephones do not provide change for unused portions of ¥100 coins. However, some (but not all) international pay phones will not let you use an NTT phonecard for international calls, since NTT (Nippon Telegraph and Telephone) is not an international carrier. In such cases, you'll need a phonecard from KDD, the dominant international telecom company. Most international pay phones provide information on international dialling and operator assistance as well as details on which international carriers are available (there are several, all offering similar charges).

Services such as credit calls, reverse-charge (collect) calls and person-to-person calls are not available for every country, so inquire beforehand. You can also dial direct from KDD (Kokusai Denshin Denwa) offices.

Mobile phones. Of the three major mobile phone companies (NTT DoCoMo, Au and Softbank), DoCoMo (tel: 0120-680-100) and Softbank (tel: 3560-7730) provide rentals for use within Japan. Alternatively, you can buy a prepay mobile phone with a Japanese SIM card.

Where's the nearest telephone?	**ichiban chikai denwa wa doka des(u) ka**	いちばん近い電話は どこですか。
I'd like to send a message by e-mail/fax.	**denshi-meeru/ fakk(u)su de messeeji o okuritain des(u) ga**	電子メール/ファックス でメッセージを送り たいんですが。
I'd like to buy a phonecard, please.	**terehon kaado o kudasai**	テレホンカードを ください。

TIME ZONES

Japan is 9 hours ahead of Greenwich Mean Time all year; there is no daylight savingtime. The following chart shows the time in various cities in winter:

San Francisco	New York	London	**Tokyo**	Sydney
4am	7am	noon	**9pm**	10pm

TIPPING

Tipping isn't customary (unless perhaps if you've requested an extra service) and is officially discouraged. However, a small gift – such as a souvenir of your home town – might be an appreciated gesture for people who have been exceptionally helpful. It is considered courteous to refuse gifts once or twice. Taxi drivers don't expect any tips, nor do hotel staff. Porters at airports and railway stations charge a set fee. Hotels, *ryokan* and restaurants add a 10–15 percent service charge to the bill.

TOILETS

Except in railway stations, public toilets are scarce. Use the facilities in department stores, which are generally Western-style, as are those in the big hotels. Japanese-style toilets are floor-level and lack seats: you squat facing the flush. The door usually locks, but it's customary to give two taps on the door to see if the toilet's occupied; if you're inside, you give two taps back. Public toilets are often shared by men and women (men at the urinals are supposed to be ignored). Toilets in Japan are kept scrupulously clean. It's wisest always to carry tissues with you.

Where are the toilets?	**toire wa doko des(u) ka**	トイレはどこですか。
Ladies	**josee**	女性
Gents	**dansee**	男性

TOURIST INFORMATION

The Japan National Tourist Organisation (JNTO) operates Tourist Information Centres (TIC) throughout Japan. There are also 16 overseas offices. It provides a wealth of information, including free maps, brochures, tour itineraries and advice on travel to and within Japan.

For recorded information on major events and entertainment, call JNTO's 24-hour Teletourist service: tel: (03) 3503-2911 in Tokyo, (075) 361-2911 in Kyoto. JNTO operates an extensive website at www.jnto.go.jp.

Tokyo: 10 fl. Tokyo Kotsu Kaikan Building, 2-10-1, Yurakucho, Chiyoda-ku, Tokyo 100-0006; tel: (03) 3201-3331.

Narita Airport: Terminal 1, tel: (0476) 30-3383; Terminal 2, tel: (0476) 34-5877.

Kyoto: 9 fl. Kyoto Station Building, Shiokoji-sagaru, Karasuma-dori, Shimogyo-ku, Kyoto; tel: (075) 344-3300.

Australia: Level 7, 36–38 Clarence Street, Sydney NSW 2000; tel: (02) 9279-2177; www.jnto.org.au.

Canada: 481 University Avenue, Suite 306, Toronto, Ontario M5G 2E9; tel: (416) 366-7140; www.jnto.go.jp/canada.
UK: 5th floor, 12/13 Nicholas Lane, London EC4N 7BN; tel: (020) 7398-5670; www.seejapan.co.uk.
US: One Rockefeller Plaza, Suite 1250, New York, NY 10020; tel: (212) 757-5640; www.japantravelinfo.com.

Where is the tourist office?	kankoo an-nai-jo doko	観光案内所はどこですか。
Do you have information on...?	...no an-nai wa arimas(u) ka	...の案内はありますか。
Are there any trips to...?	...e no tsuaa wa arimas(u) ka	...へのツアーはありますか。
How much will the trip cost?	sono tsuaa wa ikura des(u) ka	そのツアーはいくらですか。
Do you have a guidebook?	gaido-bukku wa arimas(u) ka	ガイドブックはありますか。
Can you help me?	tas(u)kete kudasai	助けてください。

TRAVELLERS WITH DISABILITIES

In general, Japan is not user-friendly for the disabled. Doors, lifts, toilets and just about everything else have not been designed for wheelchairs, nor are there any regulations regarding access for the disabled.

Forget about using a wheelchair in train or subway stations, much less trains, during rush hour. The crowds are just too thick, and too rude. To arrange assistance – in advance – at Tokyo Station, call the JR English InfoLine at (03) 3423-0111. It is possible to reserve a special seat for wheelchairs on the *shinkansen*, or bullet train. Reservations can be made from one month to two days before departure. You must also reserve ahead to use the elevators for the *shinkansen* platforms. In many stations, staff will help with escalators and lifts.

Narita Airport's website (www.narita-airport.or.jp) has information for disabled travellers. For general information about travel or help in Tokyo, call the Tell-Tokyo English Lifeline, tel: (03) 3968-4099.

W

WEBSITES

• Japan National Tourist Organisation: www.jnto.go.jp. Excellent links and travel information.

• *Japan Times*: www.japantimes.co.jp. Oldest and most important English-language daily.

• Japan Railways: www.japanrail.com. Official JR site; includes schedules, fares and information about the Japan Rail Pass.

• J Pop: www.jpop.com. Comprehensive guide to Japanese pop culture and its icons.

• Metropolis: www.metropolis.co.jp. The lowdown on Tokyo's nightlife, restaurants and events of interest.

• Subway Navigator: www.subwaynavigator.com. Good route planning guide to subways the world over.

• Sumo World: www.sumo.or.jp. Site on the giant wrestlers and their upcoming bouts.

• Tokyo Consumer Prices: www.pricechecktokyo.com. Guide to cost of living in Tokyo.

• Tokyo Food Page: www.bento.com. Good online restaurant guide.

• *Tokyo Journal*: www.tokyo.to. Good events site with entertainment, food and nightlife listings.

• *Tokyo Q*: www.tokyoq.com. One of the better on-line guides with restaurant and nightlife postings

WEIGHTS AND MEASURES

All the ancient measures have been replaced by the metric system, apart from those used for carpentry in Shinto temples and for making kimono.

INDEX

Berlitz pocket guide
Japan

Third Edition 2009
Reprinted 2010

Written by Jack Altman
Updated by Stephen Mansfield
Series Editor: Tony Halliday

Photography credits
All photography by Dennis Kessler/Berlitz
except pages: 6 by C. Huber; 10, 12, 15, 42, 43,
45, 48, 50, 62, 68, 72, 78, 81, 183, 184, 185, 191,
193, 196, 203, 204, 207 by Stephen Mansfield/
Apa; 19, 21, 22, 24, 26, 27, 34, 36 by Tokyo
National Museum; 28 by AKG; 37 by Kanagawa
Prefectural Museum; 38 by Apa; 3 (top right),
88, 133, 143, 177, 178 courtesy of JNTO; 136
by Michael Freeman/Corbis; 22, 166 by Berlitz/
Click Chicago; 182 by Ming-Tang Evans.

Cover picture: 4Corners Images

Every effort has been made to provide
accurate information in this publication,
but changes are inevitable. The publisher
cannot be responsible for any resulting
loss, inconvenience or injury.

Contact us

At Berlitz we strive to keep our guides as
accurate and up to date as possible, but if you
find anything that has changed, or if you have
any suggestions on ways to improve this guide,
then we would be delighted to hear from you.

Berlitz Publishing, PO Box 7910,
London SE1 1WE, England.
fax: (44) 20 7403 0290
email: berlitz@apaguide.co.uk
www.berlitzpublishing.com